S0-AWM-607

CONVERSATIONS *With* ERNEST

A special tribute to the life and lasting influence of Dr. Ernest Holmes

FOREWORD BY
REV. DAVID GOLDBERG, PH.D.

SPIRITUAL LIVING PRESS

Spiritual Living Press
573 Park Point Drive | Golden CO 80401-7042

Spiritual Living Press
573 Park Point Drive
Golden, CO 80401-7402
720-496-1370
www.ScienceofMind.com

Printed in the United States of America
Published October 2018

Editor: Julie Mierau
Cover Design/Book Layout:
Maria Robinson—Designs On You, LLC, Littleton CO

ISBN ebook: 978-0-917849-73-2
ISBN hardcover: 978-0-917849-74-9

Ernest was very astute
and knew when he needed to move from a dramatic
tone to a humorous one. For this moment,
he would bring out a big white handkerchief with great
exaggeration and very loudly blow his nose.
He would say,
"I knew I could get your attention some way."

"In His Company: Ernest Holmes Remembered"
by Marilyn Leo

PREFACE

*I*n these pages, a variety of contributors offer their imagined conversations between Dr. Ernest Holmes and a variety of other people, visionaries and beings. Here is a brief look at the life and work of Dr. Holmes.

Ernest Shurtleff Holmes — American New Thought writer, teacher and leader — founded the spiritual movement known as Religious Science, part of the greater New Thought movement, whose spiritual philosophy is known as the Science of Mind. He wrote the seminal work, "The Science of Mind," along with numerous other metaphysical books. He founded Guide for Spiritual Living: Science of Mind magazine, which has been in continuous publication since 1927. His books remain in print, and the principles he taught have inspired and influenced generations of metaphysical students and teachers.

Holmes was born January 21, 1887, in Lincoln, Maine. He left school and his family when he moved to Boston at the age of 15. From 1908 to 1910 he worked in a store to pay for his tuition at Boston's Leland Powers School of Expression. There he was introduced to Mary Baker Eddy's "Science and Health," as well as Christian Science.

In 1912 Holmes joined his brother Fenwicke in Venice, California. In addition to taking up a job with the city government, Holmes and his brother, a Congregationalist minister, studied the writings of Thomas Troward, Ralph Waldo Emerson, William Walker Atkinson and Christian D. Larson.

After leading small private meetings throughout the city, in 1916 Ernest Holmes was invited to speak at the Metaphysical Library in Los Angeles. This led him to repeat engagements and a nationwide tour. In 1919 he published his first book, "The Creative Mind," and after almost a decade of touring he committed to remaining in the L.A. area to complete his major work, "The Science of Mind," published in 1926. In 1927, he married Hazel Durkee Foster.

That year Holmes started speaking each Sunday morning in a theater in the Ambassador Hotel that seated 625. In November 1927, he moved to the 1,295-seat Ebell Theatre. As his reach continued to expand, in February 1927, he incorporated the Institute of Religious Science and School of Philosophy, Inc., and later that year he began publishing Science of Mind magazine. In 1935 he reincorporated his organization as the Institute of Religious Science and Philosophy, and in 1954 it was reestablished again as a religious organization called the Church of Religious Science.

He died on April 7, 1960.

Today his Science of Mind/Religious Science principles continue to spread through the Centers for Spiritual Living, Association for Global New Thought, Affiliated New Thought Network, Global Religious Science Ministries, independent Religious Science ministries and other organizations.

FOREWORD

Rev. Dr. David Goldberg

The annual retreat was one of the rituals of ministerial school that I enjoyed the most. This particular retreat was the best. We came together to deepen our connection with Spirit and our bonds with each other while we honored our graduating seniors and our teachers. Along with rich spiritual practices, we also had a lot of fun, including during one of our mixers at the end of a long day. We all wore our version of PJs, whether silk robes or sweat pants, and spent time dancing, singing, eating and just being together.

During this particular celebration, one of our classmates displayed a previously unknown gift: that of impersonating our founder, Dr. Ernest Holmes. Darrell Jones spontaneously entered into a conversation between Holmes and another being.

David Goldberg

If I had closed my eyes, I would have sworn that Ernest was in the room. Darrell had the depth and breadth of knowledge, wisdom and information to continue for more than five minutes, having us laughing hysterically because every aspect was just so good.

As we continued in school and eventually graduated, I always remembered how now Rev. Darrell was able to entertain and educate by sharing his gifts in such a unique way. I offer my thanks to Darrell for planting the seed for "Conversations with Ernest."

We shared the idea with our readers of Guide for Spiritual Living: Science of Mind magazine more than two years ago. The invitation was for you to put someone you know, or would like to know, in conversation with Ernest Holmes. As the minister to those who read the magazine, my strategy was for you to take a deeper dive into the work of Dr. Holmes.

We heard from dozens of you, and the result is the book you are holding. I learned a tremendous amount about Dr. Holmes and so many other sages and wisdom keepers, both known and unknown to me. Thank you for your authenticity and openness in sharing your stories, whether based in fiction or reality. I am grateful for your extraordinary creativity.

In the following pages you will find a myriad of stories and conversations in several different styles. We chose to leave them mainly as written, offering only minor editing for clarity.

In addition to all of the enlightening voices and ideas from so many writers, we also wanted to bring you some of the brilliant work of Dr. Holmes himself. As an added benefit, our bonus section is a reprint of Holmes' last sermon, "Sermon by the Sea," which he delivered in the Chapel at Asilomar State Park in California in 1959. He made his transition one year later. This sermon stirs my soul, and I lovingly share it with you as a part of this book.

If you feel so moved, please complete your own unique conversation with Ernest between Dr. Holmes and someone important in your life. Look for the guidelines at www.ScienceofMind.com, write it up, send it to us, and your story may appear in the next edition of "Conversations With Ernest." And while you're on our site, sign up for our free, bi-monthly newsletter that expands on some stories in the print and electronic versions of the magazine and offers some additional content. As well, while you're online, be sure to "like" Science of Mind magazine on Facebook and join the conversation with almost 500,000 like-minded beings.

As Holmes wrote in "The Art of Life," "You do not have to beseech Life to be good or to bring good into your life. Life is like the sun. It shines on everything. Get out of the shadows! Crawl out of your basement! Open the windows of your mind! Open the doors of your soul! Lift up your thought, and let Life be to you whatever you wish It to be! Learn to resurrect yourself!"

I trust that, in some small way, this book will help you do just that.

With Great Love,

Rev. Dr. David Goldberg
Publisher, Spiritual Living Press
September 30, 2018
Golden, Colorado

There was an openness about Holmes to be admired, and he was not too concerned about the mores of our society except as to how you thought and believed in your own life. When Holmes was a Boy Scout troop leader, he took a group of young men on a camping trip. It must have been in the Northern California area because Holmes had a speaking engagement in San Francisco that coincided with the camping trip.

Immediately following the experience in the woods, Holmes was to speak in an auditorium. There had been some delay in his arrival, and the people in the audience were becoming restless, wondering where their beloved speaker was. Finally, Holmes arrived.

Not having had time to change into more "respectable" clothes, he entered from the main door and onto the platform in his scouting uniform, short pants and all. He was not embarrassed or concerned. He was there to share his ideas about life, and it did not matter what he was wearing.

Marilyn Leo
October 2017 issue, Guide for Spiritual Living:
Science of Mind magazine

ACKNOWLEDGMENTS

Thank you to all of the readers of Guide for Spiritual Living: Science of Mind magazine who accepted the invitation to put Dr. Ernest Holmes into conversation with someone in their lives, known or unknown, for a deeper look into the consciousness and personality of the founder of Religious Science. Dr. Holmes was the first to state that we accept wisdom wherever it lies, whether with the known mystics, with yourself or with a dog named Bella.

This book, in words and graphics, is a direct result of the extra-ordinary talent and amazing consciousness of Julie Mierau and Maria Robinson, respectively. You are amazing beings, and thank you for shining your light so selflessly and brilliantly.

We are indebted to the Science of Mind Archives and Library's Executive Director Rev. Kathy Mastroianni for providing photos of Ernest Holmes.

Science of Mind Publishing, in the form of Holli Sharp, Associate Editor & Creative Director; Tony Lobato, Advertising Sales Coordinator; and Kari Johnson, Publishing Business Administrator, is a powerful written word ministry of the Centers for Spiritual Living. You do so much for so many each and every day. We are so grateful for your service.

The Executive Team and the Leadership Council continue to set the bar high with regard to how we take this teaching to the world. Thank you to Rev. Dr. Kenn Gordon, Spiritual Leader; Rev. Sharon Hudson, Field Leader; Tracy Brown, RScP, Leadership Council Chair; and Mr. Steve Burton, Executive Director, Centers for Spiritual Living; as well as all of the volunteer members of the Leadership Council and all of our councils, committees and commissions for your servant leadership.

The Editorial Advisory Committee of Centers for Spiritual Living continues to bring their expertise and consciousness to all we do and all we are. We offer our thanks to Dr. Crystal Davis, Rev. Dr. Joel Fotinos, Rev. Patrick Harbula, Rev. Robyn Holt, Ben Jamison, RScP, and Dr. Joni Samples. Your service is exemplary and heartfelt.

To all of the writers, columnists and contributors to Science of Mind magazine past and present, thank you for sharing your unique voice and interpretation of the Divine with our tens of thousands of readers. Whether you have written for the magazine for months or decades, we are grateful.

You continue to allow us to be a part of your spiritual journey. It is a high honor and a ministry we take seriously. From the top of my overflowing heart, thank you.

Rev. Dr. David Goldberg, Publisher

TABLE OF CONTENTS

A CONVERSATION WITH...

CONVERSATIONS *With* ERNEST

Preserving the Legacy of Dr. Holmes

by KATHY MASTROIANNI

A Conversation with Kathy Mastroianni

REVEREND KATHY MASTROIANNI is a Centers for Spiritual Living minister. She is the executive director of the Science of Mind Archives and Library.

KATHY MASTROIANNI Hi, Ernest. It certainly is an honor to meet and talk with you in person — though in reality we talk daily while I am at work.

ERNEST HOLMES Likewise, Kathy. I so appreciate all your work for the Science of Mind Archives.

KM I enjoy being a part of preserving the timeless wisdom that is housed here, much of which Dr. Marilyn Leo has helped to collect.

EH Ah, Marilyn. I remember her and Dorothy when they were little girls coming over to see Hazel and me at our home. You know we were neighbors and her father, Reginald, was a close protégé and friend of mine. Lovely, inquisitive children.

KM I did hear about that, Ernest. And thanks to Dr. Marilyn, we have these important archives where we have fascinating pieces of history of how you founded the Science of Mind movement. We even have some of your handwritten manuscripts from when you and Fenwicke wrote your last book, "The Voice Celestial."

EH Oh? You have those? Chicken scratch, really. Fen and I would go back and forth allowing Spirit to talk through us, and I work best when I write things down. God bless

Helen, my secretary, for being able to read my scribbles and type them up into some form that made sense.

KM Agreed, I've seen them! Do you know, Ernest, when I give tours of the archives, that of all the photographs, notes, poetry, rare books and more that are lovingly preserved here, what the most treasured and favorite item of all is?

EH No, Kathy, I don't. What on earth could it be?

KM Your plaid shirt.

EH The Pendleton? Well, it certainly was a favorite of mine. Comfortable, really, and why should we go around all the time in suits and ties? God loves us and knows our truth however we show up — even in a plaid shirt.

KM I look forward to connecting with you and your teachings on a deeper and deeper level, Ernest.

EH Yes, that One Mind is ever-present, and please know that my soul and spirit are ever-expanding and ever-evolving through each and every one who takes these teachings to heart and puts them to work in their own lives.

KM Thank you for your time, Ernest. See you at work tomorrow.

Holmes was called "Happy" by local children, and he was completely uninhibited and at ease on the platform or around others. One Sunday, he was lecturing at the Beverly Theater. In the middle of his talk, at a dramatic point in his message, he paused, looked down and started chuckling. Then to the audience, he said, "I guess you are all wondering what I'm laughing about. Probably none of you know except Hazel. It just occurred to me that I have on two suits. I have the pants to one suit and the coat to another suit."

Marilyn Leo, October 2017 issue,
Guide for Spiritual Living:
Science of Mind magazine

Celebrating Our Inherent Divine Dignity

by MERRILYN RICHARDSON

A Conversation with Edgar Cayce

MERRILYN RICHARDSON IMAGINES AN ENCOUNTER between Ernest Holmes and Edgar Cayce, known as "The Sleeping Prophet," a rural southern Sunday School teacher and medical intuitive. According to New Thought historian Mitch Horowitz, both men transcended the prejudices of their day because of their belief in — and experience of — people's inherent Divine dignity.

ERNEST HOLMES Edgar, your psychic readings have revealed some amazing knowledge and have helped many seekers of truth and healing. But some would say you should never allow another entity to control your mind.

EDGAR CAYCE That's not what happens in my case. You see, when I'm in an altered state of consciousness, my individual mind reads the individual mind of the seeker. No other person, alive or dead, speaks through me.

EH Great! That's another example of the evidence of the oneness in all humanity.

EC Yes, however, in this three-dimensional Earth that we inhabit, we express as spirit, mind and body. I have a saying: Spirit is the Life, Mind is the builder, and the physical is the result.

EH That's wonderful. Metaphysical teachings interpret the Christ as the Mind of God individualized. As I've written, it's the study of Life and the Nature of Law, governed and directed by thought; always conscious that we live in a spiritual Universe; that God is in, through, around and for us. ... That which today seems to us supernatural, after it is thoroughly understood, will be found spontaneously natural.

EC True, it is a spiritual universe, and what we call solid forms, when analyzed, are pure energy or atoms in motion. In other words, God. I've said it before: The Earth is only an atom in the universe.

EH That ties in with what Dr. Deepak Chopra found when studying his native Hindu heritage. While scientists say atoms are formed by neutrons and protons floating around in empty space, Chopra says the space is not empty but full of consciousness.

EC See, mind is the builder, or as some modern seekers say, it is directive intelligence.

EH I've said it this way: The most precious thing a man possesses is his own Individuality; indeed this is the only thing he really has — or is. For one instant to allow any outside influence to enter or control this individuality is a crime against his real self.

EC I believe there are astrological influences as a portion of everyone's experience, but we have a choice in whether to be guided by such. First things first: know in whom and what you believe spiritually. As the law of the Lord says: Love God with all of your mind, body and soul and your neighbor, friend or foe as yourself.

Our choices must take into consideration the problems of the homeless, jobless and hungry. The gift for entering into Life can be an opportunity for each soul to express its gratitude for Life and its expressions from the bounties of the Creator.

EH We understand that the life of all is God.

"The truth about the nature of Divine Reality,
to the extent that it is known to man,
is not a revelation of any one person or of any
particular age. It is rather a result of the hope, the aspiration and
the effort of all people in all ages."

Dr. Ernest Holmes,
foreword to the 1938 edition of "The Science of Mind"

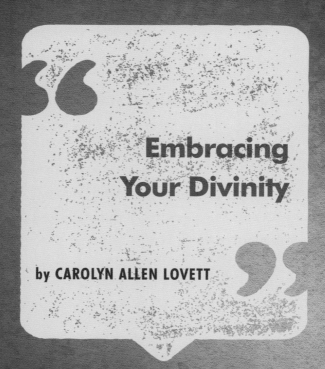

Embracing Your Divinity

by CAROLYN ALLEN LOVETT

A Conversation with Carolyn Allen Lovett

IT WAS A SPLENDID SUNDAY MORNING: sunny, cumulus clouds dotted the clear-blue sky and, although hot and humid, the car's air conditioner kept undesirable elements at bay. A perfect day for driving home from a weekend family celebration.

I watched from the passenger's seat as we whizzed by Georgia's country homes flanked by a seeming infinity of oaks and pines—all comfortably tucked in the shadows of Atlanta. I was startled from my musing by "The Voice" — not my companion from the driver's seat. "Embrace your divinity!" Clear, calm but commanding, the message delivered in an instant. I'd heard The Voice before. Its pronouncements are rare, but each time it surprises me.

Later, watching the sunset disappear over the horizon, I wondered what the urgent directive meant. In the stillness of that summer evening, Ernest Holmes delivered the answer, from the pages of his book, "The Science of Mind."

"God's Creative Power of Mind is right here," Holmes said. "We have as much of this power to use as we believe in and embody."

I remembered the section — "The Power Within" — from my dog-eared copy of the textbook. Apparently, I read Holmes' teachings better than I practiced them.

Holmes continued, "We set our own limitations. The Prodigal Son remained a prodigal as long as he chose to do so. When he chose to, he returned to his 'Father's house' and was greeted with outstretched hands. So shall our experience be when we return to the world which is perfect; there will be something which will turn to us. We shall behold a new heaven and a new earth, not in some far-off place but here and now."

Holmes had decoded the message: Nothing is holding me back. I can embrace the truth of my divinity and live my life full force, without limitations. I can embody the Power Within. I must choose.

The Voice's command had sounded urgent — no choice involved. Ignoring it didn't seem to be an option. But there is a choice. Always.

Now, the hard part: actually embracing my divinity — every day, in all situations.

"In a world that moves at a whirlwind pace and seems more impersonal and unpredictable each day, how do I live my divinity?" I asked.

Not to worry, Holmes had an answer for that, too.

"Do you remember 'Spiritual Mind Healing,' Part Three of my book?"

Of course not, at least not specifically, I mused.

"Read it again," he suggested. "It's all about practice, the technique by which we lay hold of mind power and prove its practicability."

Holmes paused. "Part Two is 'Spiritual Mind Healing ... Ideation.' Seems we humans prefer to dwell in ideation ... much easier to read about it and talk about it than to practice it. Practice being your God-self — your divinity."

Holmes thrust his arms toward me and chuckled. "Embrace it!"

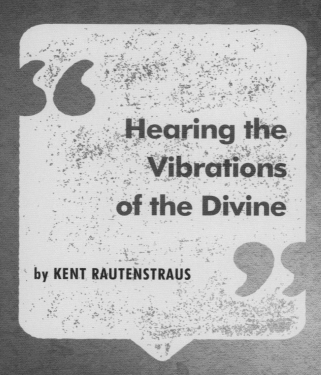

" Hearing the Vibrations of the Divine "

by KENT RAUTENSTRAUS

A Conversation with Wolfgang Amadeus Mozart

COULD THERE BE A MORE FASCINATING person for our founder, Dr. Ernest Holmes, to converse with than Wolfgang Amadeus Mozart, child prodigy, musical genius and third best-selling classical composer of all time? We know that Holmes and his wife Hazel liked classical music. No doubt, they listened to Mozart's music and heard the transcendent vibrations of the Divine. In the imagined conversation here, actual quotes from the two men are shown in italics.

ERNEST HOLMES Wolfgang Amadeus Mozart, your music is sublime! I'm sure you agree that *the greatest music ever composed was written by the hand of a mystic, and the highest and best in art has come from men of spiritual perception.*

WOLFGANG AMADEUS MOZART Thank you, Dr. Holmes, but may I say, *I pay no attention whatever to anybody's praise or blame. I simply follow my own feelings. I choose such notes that love one another. If only the whole world could feel the power of harmony.*

EH That is a profound statement. Infinite Love harmonizes man's entire being.

WM Love, love, love — that is the soul of genius!

EH Yes! Pulsations of life are governed by Love! Tell me, Mr. Mozart, or may I call you Wolfgang?

WM Call me Wolfie, everyone else does.

EH Okay, Wolfie. How do you receive inspiration?

WM Actually, *when I am traveling in a carriage, or walking after a good meal, or during the night when I cannot sleep, it is on such occasions that ideas flow best and most abundantly.*

EH Fascinating! *A power greater than I am flows through me into everything I do or think about. I know that at all times I have a silent partner walking with me, talking with me, operating through me.*

WM You're plugged in, my friend.

EH Well I believe that *the possibilities of my experience are unlimited.* But, Wolfie, how do you download the music in your soul?

WM *You know that I immerse myself in music, so to speak — that I think about it all day long — that I like experimenting, studying, reflecting. Music is my life, and my life is music. I tell you, when I am at peace with myself, then thoughts flow into me most easily and at their best. And what I've really learned is that the music is not in the notes, but in the silence between.*

EH *Sweet song of the silence, forever singing in my heart!*

WM Dr. Holmes, *to talk well and eloquently is a very great art, but an equally great one is to know the right moment to stop.* Now, I have to write the Jupiter Symphony before dinner, but I do have a final question for you. Do you have nickname, like Ernest or Ernie?

EH Call me Dr. Holmes.

Healing Our World

by JODI BUSHDIECKER

A Conversation with Pope Francis

IN THIS IMAGINED CONVERSATION BETWEEN ERNEST HOLMES

AND POPE FRANCIS, the italicized portions are direct quotes from

these luminaries.

POPE FRANCIS In my Encyclical Letter, "Laudato Si' — On Care For Our Common Home," I share my concern about the ecological condition of the Earth, and I call for individuals and faith communities around the globe to heal the Earth through spiritual renewal. The underlying theological conviction of the Encyclical is that everything in the world is connected in the web of life, and God's love is the foundation of existence.

ERNEST HOLMES Religious Scientists affirm the unity of Life. God is the One Life, and we are One with the Whole. We understand God as Love and Law.

POPE My concerns for ecology and justice are grounded in the intimate relationship between the poor and the fragility of the planet. I also have concerns about technology, consumerism and practices of our modern throw-away culture that do not honor life and relationship to God, others and nature.

EH The outward life is a result of the subjective state of thought. Humans are microcosms of Spirit. We create our own experience through our beliefs. Suffering is not ordained by God but rather is the result of an infringement on the Laws of the Universe. Conditions such as poverty lack, and limitation are not in principle or law but only in the individual use we make of principle.

POPE I re-define the traditional interpretation of humanity's domin-ion over the Earth to be one of right relationship with God, others and nature. I call humanity to the tremendous responsibility for creation that is grounded in the intimate connection among all crea-tures and the fact that *the natural environment is a collective good, the patrimony of all humanity and the responsibility of everyone.*

EH Our hope lies in knowing the Truth. The process of healing our Earth is to change our thinking through consciousness of our unity with the Whole, through conscious cooperation with the law and through creation of a mental equivalent of perfection, wholeness and harmony for our Earth home. This is what is meant by right relationship — or constructive use of the law — or cosmic consciousness.

EH *The Spirit of God has filled the universe with possibilities and therefore, from the very heart of things, something new can always emerge.* I believe that technological solutions to environmental issues must respect the rights of people and cultures around the globe, and I advocate for a preferential option for the poor and disenfranchised. I also call for dialogue that brings forth honest debate among leaders at the international, national and local levels — and for simplicity of living that re-examines our definition of progress in human relationships.

EH All problems are solved through the power of right thinking. The way to deal with the environmental crisis is through an evolution of consciousness. Healing of the natural world will occur through the inner realization of perfect God, perfect humanity, perfect Earth.

AP PHOTO/GREGORIO BORGIA

Living From Divine Purpose

by NANCY FAGEN

A Conversation with Ella Wheeler Wilcox

DR. ERNEST HOLMES AND ELLA Wheeler Wilcox, both influential New Thought leaders, meet in this imaginary conversation. Wilcox's most enduring work is the poem "Solitude," which includes the lines "Laugh, and the world laughs with you; Weep, and you weep alone; For the sad old earth must borrow its mirth, But has trouble enough of its own." Direct quotations from these two spiritual leaders are shown in italics.

ERNEST HOLMES Ms. Wilcox, let me introduce myself. I am Ernest Holmes, and I am pleased to let you know that I admire your writings. I congratulate you for having a distribution of 50,000 copies of your booklet "What I Know About New Thought."

ELLA WHEELER WILCOX Thank you Dr. Holmes. I think the world is also ready for "The Heart of The New Thought," that I published in 1902. As I noted in that work, I am all goodness, love, truth, mercy, health. *I am a necessary part of God's universe. I am a divine soul, and only good can come through me or to me. God made me, and He could make nothing but goodness and purity and worth. I am the reflection of all His qualities. This is the new religion; yet it is older than the universe. It is God's own thought put into practical form.*

EH I agree. In the foreword of "The Science of Mind" I wrote, *I do not claim to have discovered any new Truth. The truth has been known in every age by a few; but the great mass of people has never even dreamed that we live in a mental and spiritual world. Today, however, there is a great inquiry into the deeper meaning of life because the race has reached a state of unfoldment where a broader scope is possible.*

EWW Yes, I believe *there is a divine purpose in your being on earth. Think of yourself as necessary to the great design. Let me suggest … you do not associate with pessimists. If you are unfortunate enough to be the son or daughter, husband or wife of one, put cotton (either real or spiritual) in your ears, and shut out the poison words of discouragement and despondency. Never feel that it is your duty to stay closely and continuously in the atmosphere of the despondent. You might as well think it your duty to stay in deep water with one who would not make the least effort to swim. Get on shore and throw out a lifeline, but do not remain and be dragged under. You would not permit the dearest person on earth to administer slow poison to you if you knew it.*

EH This is so true! Thank you for blessing the world with your New Thought writings.

Learning About God's Love

by FOSTER HARDING

A Conversation with Foster Harding

OUR CHURCH WAS FULL when we arrived so we had front row seats. Dad didn't like that but Mother said we had to stay. We just sat down when our minister introduced Dr. Ernest Holmes, and he walked to the podium. He was quite short and stood to the side so people could see him better. Despite being in the front row and his big voice filling our small church, my 7-year-old mind was soon wandering.

Suddenly Dr. Holmes pointed at me. "You there in the front row – what's your name?"

"Me?"

"Yes you with the curly blond hair. What's your name?"

"Uhh ... my name is Foster."

"Foster – that's a special sounding name – maybe you'll be famous some day. Would you come up here with me?"

"Up there?"

"Yes, right up here with me."

I looked at Mom. She nodded, so I climbed the steps and stood next to him.

"Foster, do you know that God loves you?"

"Me? I don't think so. I know Jesus loves me, but God is mad at me because I'm a sinner."

He seemed surprised, "Well Foster, where did you get that idea?"

"Last month an evangelist said we were all born sinners because a big snake made Adam and Eve ate fruit from the wrong tree — and God got so mad He chased them away and has been mad at all of us ever since. He said God wants to send us to hell."

He smiled and rumpled my curly locks. "Wow, Foster."

Then he knelt down beside me on one knee, and looked right in my eyes, "Here is the truth about God and about you, Foster. God loves you. God loves you more than you could ever imagine. He loves you so much He lives right in there with you."

Dr. Holmes was tapping gently right over my heart. "God and you are kind of one thing. He is so much a part of you, that when you breathe, God is breathing right along with you. When God's heart beats it is so close it's like you are sharing the same heart. That's how much God loves you. When you go home tonight please remember that for me. And when you wake up tomorrow, remember what I've said – God loves you.

"When you are happy and having fun, God is having fun, too. And, Foster, God has already given you everything you need to live your dreams. Everything – it's all right there inside of you."

He looked deep into my eyes and concluded with, "Bless you, my boy, bless you, and thanks for helping me tell these people about God's love."

Then he gave me a big hug before I ran back to Mommy and Daddy. All the people were clapping because he had made my heart very, very happy.

"Awakening to Your Spiritual Magnificence"

by LORETTA BROOKS

A Conversation with Jean Houston

Editor's Note: The following is printed with permission from Jean Houston, who shares this brief anecdote. "When I was 9 years old, my mother took me to listen to one of Ernest Holmes sermons and afterwards I shook hands with that fine gentleman who, as I recall, was quite merry."

HEAR TWO GREAT LUMINARIES having an imaginary conversation; open your hearts, open your minds. Direct quotes are shown in italics.

ERNEST HOLMES I understand you wrote the foreword to our most recent publication of "Science of Mind." I have an extraordinary respect for you, Jean, and the way you embody the principles of our work. I love the way you capture the essence of our teaching. The highest God and the innermost God is one God. This captures not only the essence but the practice of Oneness.

As I stated in the "Science of Mind," *God's creative power of mind is right here. We have as much of this power to use as we believe in and embody.*

JEAN HOUSTON It was a privilege to write the foreword for the "Science of Mind" text. *It is perhaps one of the most potent and influential books of the 20th century. Its words have inspired countless millions, seeded the growth of spiritually innovative churches and philosophies, yet no university places it in its curriculum. Perhaps this is as it should be for it is the hidden masterpiece which must be discovered only when one is ready to enter upon the larger life.*

EH I could not have said this better myself, Jean. I am grateful and pleased that so many people are awakening to their spiritual magnificence. Do keep up the good work and remember, *within us is the unborn possibility of limitless experience. Ours is the privilege of giving birth to it.*

JH Thanks for the encouraging words. I am reminded of a quote from Sir Isaac Newton, "If I have seen further than others, it is because I have stood on the shoulders of giants."

Jean Houston

Dear Ernest, you are one of those giants upon whose shoulders we all stand. As I say in my book "The Wizard of Us": The time has come for each of us to dare enter the inner sanctum of our own power, to stroll defiantly past the smoke and mirrors in order to pull back the curtain and see who is really pulling all of the controls. We are creating it all. For the true Wizard is us. Remember the "if I only" in the Wizard of Oz. If only I had a brain, some courage, a heart. Instead of "if I only," we find ourselves on the Yellow Brick Road with our faithful allies, representations of mind, heart and courage.

Ernest, we are on one of our greatest journeys. These are the times, we are the people, and we now stand on the shoulders of Spirit, creating a world that works for everyone.

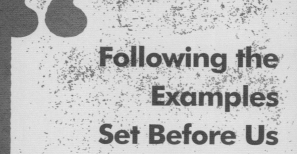

Following the Examples Set Before Us

by JAYNE GARDNER

A Conversation with Mary Magdalene

IN A CONVERSATION WITH ARGUABLY ONE OF HISTORY'S MOST INFLUENTIAL WOMEN, Ernest discusses the teaching of Jesus, gender issues and more.

ERNEST HOLMES Mary Magdalene, I am honored for the opportunity to speak with you.

MARY MAGDALENE Dr. Holmes, as I watched your life unfold from the other side, I felt an automatic kinship to you. Like me, you interpret the message of Jesus to be different than the traditional view handed down over the last 2,000 years. Does it surprise you to know that a woman was the first follower who knew the true — although secret — meaning of Jesus' message? Indeed, Christ and I were the first new thought leaders.

EH I am not surprised to find a powerful woman behind Jesus. I have to say, even though perhaps the gender expression in my writings has not shown my intention of equality, I never meant to put women in second place in any way.

MM Jesus and I were partners in developing this message. My incarnation was a rich, well-educated woman who mentored Jesus to acknowledge his gifts as powerful enough to change the world. We worked together on a body of work that was destroyed years later because of the fear it brought to the church; however, there was nothing to fear in the truths we revealed to the world.

EH My sense is that my own teachings of new thought supported the same truths. Let's compare, shall we?

MM Yes! I will start. To know oneself at the deepest level is to know the divine.

EH I believe in a direct relationship between God and man … err … God and man and woman.

MM *[laughs and then goes on]* Jesus and I are examples of what we can all become, not exceptions.

EH I so agree, and I would add that to have the same mind as Jesus implies a power that is available to all and may be used by all.

MM Instead of a Big Man up in the sky, the divine could be better described as a Big Mind, the Mind of God. We can understand it as a harmonious and dynamic relationship of the opposites of male and female, symbolized by the integrated minds of Jesus Christ and me.

EH Ahh, the Divine partnership. I love and appreciate your balance of the sexual energies. I might suggest that we are incarnations of the same field of thought.

MM Yes! I am so pleased with your work and see it as an extension of my own. I owe you a deep debt of gratitude for furthering Jesus' and my teachings.

EH We are a part of the very act of reincarnation itself, of Divine Intelligence, expanding by successive degrees of incarnation. That evolution of the human mind links us together.

MM Oh, Ernest, do you mind if I call you that? I have always loved your view of God, as well as your unique use of capitalization. We must talk again soon.

EH The pleasure has been mine.

Synthesizing Commonalities

by MARK GILBERT

A Conversation with Ken Wilber

KEN WILBER, SOMETIMES CALLED the "Einstein of consciousness," is the author of multiple books. His integral philosophy has been endorsed by former U.S. President Bill Clinton and many others. Here I imagine a meeting between these two men, both driven to find what unites humanity and Spirit. Imagine the setting for this historic meetings between two renowned philosophers taking place late one afternoon in Wilber's loft overlooking downtown Denver. (We are grateful to Wilber for his assistance with this conversation.)

KEN WILBER Ernie, your Science of Mind philosophy has certainly touched the lives of many people. How did you go about creating it?

ERNEST HOLMES I have always been fascinated by the deeper questions of meaning. I can remember my brother, William, lending me a copy of a book by Emerson when I was around 20 that just set my mind on fire. From there, I went on to read everything I could get my hands on — from philosophy to science to religion. I was simply looking for truth. And I found there was a common thread running through most of the things that spoke to me.

KW I can really relate, my friend. What happened next?

EH Well, I began synthesizing these commonalities. Eventually one person asked me to come speak to his metaphysical discussion group. My ideas were well received. I began speaking more and decided to write down my ideas into books and evolved the philosophy and wrote my complete ideas in "The Science of Mind." How did you come up with your integral philosophy, Ken?

KW Very similar story. I was in college, studying science. I was going to become a doctor. But I found that science wasn't answering my more pressing questions of meaning. That's when I discovered these writers who were bringing together Eastern and Western thought — Krishnamurti, Alan Watts and others— and they just flipped my world. I read everything I could find, both in the Eastern traditions as well as Western thought, psychotherapy and the like. The more I read, the more I found myself confused because they disagreed with one another.

EH The wisest thinkers and writers can seem to be at odds. What led you to bring them together?

KW It hit me that all these smart people couldn't be totally wrong. That's when I realized that all of them, from Zen Buddhism to psychoanalysis, contained some partial truths. They were only true for addressing different types of consciousness. That led to my first book "The Spectrum of Consciousness." From there, I continued integrating different truths and growing my integral model.

EH I believe there are no finalities in any science, philosophy or religion. I stressed that we should be open at the top to change and adapt as we discover new truths and ideas.

KW Yes. If you were updating "The Science of Mind" now, what would be some of those new ideas you would incorporate?

EH I often thought that I could have stressed the importance of love more in the textbook. Love is such an important part of our spiritual path. I also really resonated with the ideas of Sri Aurobindo, his spiritual evolutionary outlook and his integral yoga. For

a time, I was reading his wonderful book, "The Life Divine," once a year.

KW Just so you know, Aurobindo was a major influence on my integral development as well.

EH Maybe it's not so much about my rewriting "The Science of Mind" as it is for those who study it to also be open to the ideas of these other teachers and incorporate those ideas into their path in their own way.

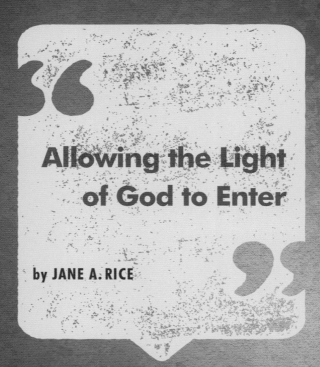

"Allowing the Light of God to Enter

by JANE A. RICE"

A Conversation with Betty Jane

AT AGE 74, Betty Jane discovered she had inflammatory breast cancer. Science of Mind magazine had been a strong source of comfort to her since she discovered the magazine many years earlier. Now she turned to it even more deeply than before. During peaceful times when she was alone, she would sometimes imagine herself talking directly to Ernest Holmes.

BETTY JANE I don't get it, Ernest. Each day I read and meditate on the Daily Guides. I find the articles informative and inspiring. And I do believe wholeheartedly that heaven is within us. Why then is cancer growing in my body?

ERNEST HOLMES Betty, while it is true that heaven is within us, we experience it to the degree that we become conscious of it. Please know that this cancer you currently and temporarily are experiencing is not some curse or form of punishment being visited upon you.

Look within your heart to find the lesson your spirit has chosen to learn. Then wake up to the cure that has always been there in your soul. You are an individualized expression of God. And God does not know dis-ease.

BJ I know these things to be true, Ernest, but still I'm afraid. Part of my body has been cut away in an attempt to save the rest of it.

EH Now, Betty, I'm not suggesting you deny your fear and pain. But you can allow yourself to be opened up by what you're experiencing. Close your eyes and breathe deeply

The life expectancy for people with inflammatory breast cancer is barely two years. Even though Betty Jane was in the latter stages when she was diagnosed, she survived nine years. She lived long enough to see all her grandchildren graduate from high school.

and slowly. Inhale good health, and exhale fear and pain. Something new will emerge from this dark place. Renewal!

BJ I think I see what you're getting at. I don't have to deny the cancer, but I don't have to hang on to it, reinforcing it.

EH Exactly, Betty. You can acknowledge what is happening, but don't be consumed by it. Allow the light of God to enter. Then, through your suffering, you can find your way home.

Ernest spent time every day right after breakfast

in his upstairs bedroom suite in meditation and treatment.

Particularly on Sunday morning,

Ernest would spend an hour or more in meditation

before giving his Sunday talk. He did a lot

of his reading and writing sitting on his bed.

Most of the Home Study Course

and "The Voice Celestial" were written in this way.

Cardboards from his laundered shirts

would serve as his writing paper.

"In His Company: Ernest Holmes Remembered"
by Marilyn Leo

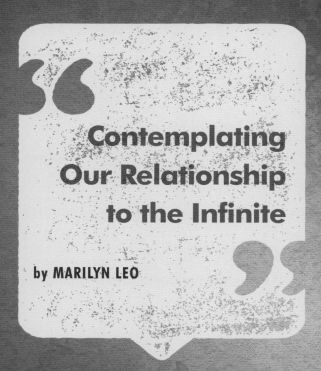

Contemplating Our Relationship to the Infinite

by MARILYN LEO

A Conversation with Ralph Waldo Emerson

Ernest Holmes credits Ralph Waldo Emerson for his first taste of philosophical thought. The following created conversation between the two draws information from Emerson's essays "Spiritual Laws" and "Nature," "A Commentary of Science of Mind" by Holmes and "The Philosophy of Emerson and Finding the Real Christ" by Holmes.

FOR THIS CONVERSATION, IMAGINE Holmes visiting Emerson in his garden in Concord, Massachusetts.

RALPH WALDO EMERSON Ah, there you are, Ernest. What a delight to have a visit with you.

ERNEST HOLMES And you, Ralph. So good to see you.

RWE Let's sit here in the garden under this tree. Isn't it a beautiful day?

EH Indeed, it is magnificent; the fragrance of the flowers and grasses is a fulfilling revelation of Spirit in all Its glory. We are so fortunate to be amongst those who recognize the truth of our being. I want to share that with everyone.

RWE Ernest, you are so very outgoing with people and are able to speak openly and freely. While I write the words I feel, you speak them outright. I am almost envious, but we each have our talent and special way to express our truth. Each of us uses the freedom we were given to express ourselves in the way we feel most comfortable.

EH Ralph, you know many years ago I suffered from a great sensitivity. It was a lack of self-confidence, and my feelings would be hurt easily. Through spiritual mind treatment I was my own first healing. With that healing came my love of people. Now I love to mingle with them and have conversations with people from all walks of life. At the same time I now spend many hours each day in meditation, keeping in close contact with that Divinity within me.

You know, Ralph, you were the first metaphysician I was exposed to. Since my teen years I have read and studied your many essays and speeches. I have come to admire you, your thoughts, philosophy and, in fact, have established practical ideas for today's seekers of truth. Are you aware that you are America's most quoted author?

RWE Well, Ernest you are very kind and seem to give me credit where it is you who must accept credit for your own desires and studies, talents and wherewithal for establishing a philosophy that is easily understood.

EH As I said, I have studied your ideas, and I have so admired your work that I wrote a small book entitled "The Philosophy of Emerson and Finding the Real Christ."

RWE That's interesting. Is it based on any particular writing?

EH As a matter of fact, yes. I used your essay "Spiritual Laws" and, perhaps most importantly, your ideas on oneness.

RWE Yes, there can be no duality in our thought or action. We cannot believe in a spiritual world in one place and a material world in another. There cannot be a God external to our souls, a heaven to be desired, an immortal existence to be obtained. If this is our thinking, it is from a standpoint of duality, not unity.

EH I trust that even to this day you hold the moments of contemplation to be as valuable as those of action.

RWE Yes, having theoretically dissolved the material universe, or having resolved it into a spiritual universe, drawing no line between cause and effect, I feel it worthwhile to contemplate my relationship to the Infinite. However, I do not completely repudiate the material world. I find prayer and performance to be two ends of the same thing. I have found in nature an answer to the call of the soul. I believe action to be good when necessary — and inaction to be equally good.

EH Ralph, I believe that each of us is here for a purpose and that we must learn to accept ourselves for better or for worse – to trust the Divine Nature inherent in our own being and to live from this Divine Nature alone.

RWE I agree. The fact that I am here certainly shows me that the soul had need of an organ here. The objective world is a necessary expression of the spirit. We would not have bodies if we did not need them, and we should not question the integrity of the soul which has projected the body.

EH As I formulate my ideas about the Divine Presence and our relationship with It, I enjoy hearing what others think. This also gives me more ideas on how to articulate principles of life as I believe them to be.

RWE Well, Ernest, I think you must be honest to yourself. I know you want to be understood by others, but as Jesus told us, those who want to hear, will – with full understanding — and others won't be ready.

EH Yes, you are right about that. I think that is one of the problems of churches today. The pompous preacher tries to cram an idea

down the throats of the congregation, and the people had better agree or they'll surely go to hell.

RWE Not everyone is so gullible. We both know that the living God will show us the way, and it is always the way of our highest good.

EH Ralph, can you imagine your voice, even your image, being broadcast to the world as you are speaking? Your words of wisdom could be heard by everyone, not just those in an auditorium.

RWE And yours, Ernest. That could be quite interesting and challenging. Would we speak as openly and earnestly as we are today? Would we still be able to enjoy the ambiance of nature? The trees and fresh air are my inspiration.

EH And mine. Hazel and I enjoy our rose garden all year round. At any rate, the radio is a voice transmitted for all to hear – if one so chooses – if the radio is turned on and tuned in. I believe it is the same with being in touch with God – with Spirit – as our intuition will guide us if and when we will listen.

RWE Indeed, our intuition is our guiding light through everyday circumstances. You know George Ripley writes about these things. He is a very active journalist and author.

EH Yes, I'm familiar with his New American Cyclopaedia and other writings.

RWE He was the man who held the first official meeting of what some called the Transcendentalist Club in his home in September 1836.

EH I rather like the nickname I've heard, "The Brotherhood of Like-Minded." Women as well as men were included in your club.

RWE Of course – there are women who take seriously our ideas and wish to voice their opinions. They are to be heard.

EH The group had brilliant ideas that were ahead of the time. They stood up for equality — against slavery and for the suffragette movement.

RWE Equality of all was probably one of the most, if not *the* most important proponent we had to offer. We certainly enjoyed those meetings.

EH In your essay "Nature" you speak eloquently on the beauty that has been created for us to simply enjoy.

RWE Yes, Ernest, it seems to me that few of us simply walk or sit and see the beauty in each star, bloom, sunset and tree. Most of us need something, an excuse, to just be with our own nature. It would be to our highest benefit and enjoyment to just sit in wonder, looking for and seeing the many gifts nature has to offer.

EH Though we are each a personification of the Infinite, each of us is different in manifestation. And yet we are identical at our root, rooted in the same unity. When asked how is it that unity can become multiplicity without division, all the great thinkers have answered it the same as you.

RWE Yes, unity never does become multiplicity; it simply personifies itself in infinite variations, but it is always unity.

EH So each of us looks different and acts differently so that unity may be expressed. We are absolutely one in Spirit and undifferentiated in Spirit. The differentiation is objective; it is in the eye of the beholder.

RWE You are right, Ernest. Since each of us is in an undifferentiated state as part of that Universal Wholeness, from that viewpoint there is neither separation nor differentiation, but variation, the multiplicity, the many, always rooted in the One.

EH Ralph, this has been a most stimulating conversation. I think we are the fortunate ones who have come to know and understand the Divine Presence. Thank you for sharing your time with me.

RWE Thank you for coming Ernest. I, too, have enjoyed our time together.

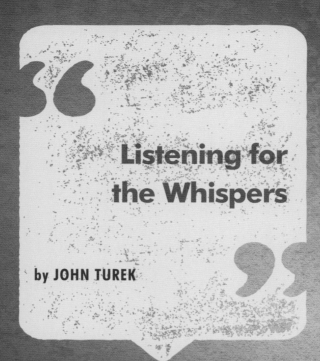

Listening for the Whispers

by JOHN TUREK

A Conversation with John Turek

AS I WONDER WHAT CONVERSATION I MIGHT HAVE with Ernest Holmes, I think about how he might encourage me to listen for the whispers.

JOHN TUREK I have a companion, an inner voice that comes forward when I'm quiet. Where does it come from?

ERNEST HOLMES Behind our humanity lies the Divine — your essence, your conscious connection to your God.

JT He seems an infrequent visitor. Why doesn't he talk with me more often?

EH Most of the time you're not listening.

JT How would you advise I become a better listener?

EH Practice!

JT Is there a best way to practice?

EH Find time for stillness. In the stillness lies the silence. In the silence, your essence whispers.

JT Then, when I'm still I can hear the whisper?

EH You are now practicing the Presence. It's simple, but it's not easy. That's all there is.

Building the Community of Our Destiny

by JEFFREE COLRBROOK

A Conversation with The Farer

IN THIS IMAGINED CONVERSATION The Farer — the traveler, the wayfarer — discusses with Ernest Holmes our mission at this time in our evolution.

THE FARER I have witnessed within the illumination of my being and within our soulmates present now on Earth an awakening to the presence of the voice celestial that speaks to our willing hearts and minds. My question to you is what should our mission now be?

ERNEST HOLMES While the greater mission has never changed — the awakening of our souls within humanity as the hologram of its creator — now the hand of eternal progress is brushing the cobwebs from the corridors of time and is again revealing to the human race the mysteries of being. There is a power in and through all that is working this great transformation. All that will not measure up to the standard must fall by its own weight. Ignorance must vanish, and understanding must be ushered in.

FARER I hear you speak and share your vision, but this time in our evolution seems to evoke the question of what action we should be engaged in now.

EH Continue to open minds and hearts to each other. Your path to this point will have allowed you to shed much unnecessary ego. Continue to bring your shadow into the light. Allow to heal that which separates us so we can work together collectively to build the new community we are destined to create.

FARER While I see many signs of the emergence of the new community, can this future world take hold in the shadow of the world now being manifested?

EH You asked what your mission should be and that is to stand fearless and seek the truth that has been veiled by fear and greed. As peaceful warriors of the universal consciousness armed with wisdom and truth and fueled by love and passion for oneness with Creator, a foothold is assured.

FARER It seems to me that the army of souls sent into the battle for the enlightenment of humanity have easily been repelled by the few free-willed people who have chosen separation and disconnectedness. The few seem to continue to grow ever larger and larger, using fear and feeding the multitudes a diet of materialism as the goal of life.

How then can you convince us that we will be able to birth a new world order other than the one planned by the existing consciousness?

EH Birthing is not without pain. We have been blessed with the light knowing itself as light. To come to this, light had to evolve to greater and greater complexity to provide a home for self-aware consciousness. It is said that the meek shall inherit the Earth, and with that humble meekness we are able to freely connect with each other as we prepare to come out of the shadow. As midwifes of the coming age, your mission is to prepare your communities to withstand this birthing with as little pain as possible.

FARER But if God is the love within my heart, having been created as eternal souls, our victory must be assured. Why would I need to enter the fray? Can you not guarantee God's victory for human evolution into Oneness consciousness?

EH A choice cannot be guaranteed. What we can say is that whatever is not of the light will not survive. Consciousness that does not reflect the light will become extinct. Humanity has the will to choose. Your eternal soul has been sent to bring the light into humanity, and I will offer you this: All of heaven stands with you and can be called on. And know you are loved.

Come Together, Over Me

by TEMPLE HAYES

A Conversation with John Lennon

IN THIS POWERFUL CONVERSATION Dr. Ernest Holmes and John Lennon — two thought-provoking creative intellectuals who believed deeply in the intrinsic value of positive thought and its profound effects on peace and happiness — come together to help us make sense of a complicated world. The italicized portions are direct quotes.

ERNEST HOLMES I've always appreciated your music and your idealism. Especially in "All You Need Is Love" and "Imagine," where you crystallized your vision for world peace. Both songs echo Science of Mind teachings because we believe *love is within us. It cannot be destroyed. It can be ignored. To the extent that we abandon love, we will feel it has abandoned us. Denying love is our only problem, and embracing it is the only answer. Through the power of love, we can let go of past history and begin again.*

Love heals, forgives and makes whole.

JOHN LENNON And I appreciate you, because I know you, like me, are a dreamer. You understand heaven and hell are states of mind and you, too, imagine that if we all joined together and lived life fully, we could live in this world as one.

If we could just get people to understand that *there are two basic motivating forces: fear and love. When we are afraid, we pull back from life. When we are in love, we open to all that life has to offer with passion, excitement and acceptance. We need to learn to love ourselves first, in all our glory and our imperfections. If we cannot love ourselves, we cannot fully open to our ability to love others or our potential to create. Evolution and all hopes for a better world rest in the fearlessness and open-hearted vision of people who embrace life.*

EH Loving yourself is the golden thread of truth found in all faith paths and it is our collective mission — as ministers, artists and individuals — to spread. *True imagination is not fanciful daydreaming; it is fire from heaven. ... Life is not just something to be endured. It is to be lived in joy, in a fullness without limit.*

JL *When I was 5 years old, my mother always told me that happiness was the key to life. When I went to school, they asked me what I wanted to be when I grew up. I wrote down "happy." They told me I didn't understand the assignment, and I told them they didn't understand life.*

EH Your mother was correct. To understand life you must understand *you belong to the universe in which you live, you are one with the Creative Genius back of this vast array of ceaseless motion, this original flow of life. You are as much a part of it as the sun, the earth and the air. There is something in you telling you this — like a voice echoing from some mountain top of inward vision.*

JL And we must believe that inward vision. *Things aren't out of our control. I still believe in love, peace. I still believe in positive thinking. While there's life, there's hope.*

Living as Infinite Spirit Beings

by CAROL WINICUR

A Conversation with Albert Einstein

IMAGINE THE FOLLOWING CONVERSATION TAKING place on a plane beyond the human body life.

ALBERT EINSTEIN Ah, Ernest Holmes. I have heard you might help me.

ERNEST HOLMES Professor Einstein, I am honored to have time with you. What concerns you?

AE For years I worked to develop a unified field theory. I wanted a complete, elegant, unassailably integrated scheme for the organization of the cosmos. I never believed in a God, at least none that any religion claimed to know. Heaven and hell were nothing but fantasies. I believed in my very bones that mankind made up a divinity because, at bottom, everyone was afraid of the dark, afraid of ultimate extinction, afraid to face the fact that individual lives meant nothing in the grand scheme of a vast and utterly indifferent cosmos.

EH But weren't you the one who said, "God does not play dice with the universe. The cosmos cannot simply be a game, designed at random and made without reason"?

AE Yes, and I also said that perhaps God is playing some other game, one we don't know yet, with rules we can't understand. Anyway, whatever I said, it was often misinterpreted.

EH Let me propose that the unified field you sought does exist. Only one power really exists — the power of God, or Universal Conscious Intelligence. God is energy. God is the love that creates all things. God is the intelligence within and through all, and God is the substance from which all is made. As to heaven and hell, you are partly correct. Heaven and hell are states of consciousness, the result of what we believe.

AE I kept looking for a simple pattern to everything. I was often asked to expound upon God, as if physics could reveal not just natural laws but a divine plan behind them. What you say makes sense, but I still wish to find the mathematics that describe this pattern.

EH There is a law in the universe that operates according to the tendency set in motion — and does so mathematically, inexorably. The Infinite Thinker thinks, and what follows is in a sequence of law and order, of cause and effect; this *is* the mathematics. The Law of Mind, or Spirit, is not different from the laws of chemistry and physics. Metaphysics begin where physics leave off. Everything is movement; all things in the physical world of form are in a certain rate of vibration and are an effect — the result of an Infinite Thinker thinking mathematically.

AE Just so, just so. On a slightly different subject, I never did fear death because I accepted my place — minuscule as an atom, insignificant as a mayfly — in a mystery and a miracle beyond full comprehension. It was enough to have participated in it and to have achieved as much as I could while there. Now, I wonder about that, too. How miniscule are we? And, as you know, I helped to create a weapon that wreaked havoc on a scale never before seen, nor even contemplated. But I was a committed pacifist. I still ask myself if I served mankind as an angel or a devil.

EH Atomic power always existed. You helped harness that which is really a neutral power. You served mankind as neither angel nor devil. It is used, constructively or destructively, depending on the intention of those who use it. I think you can agree with me that we are living an expanded life now, and our new life is a great adventure. Our bodies were miniscule and fleeting. But the most real thing about us was and always will be that we are infinitely huge Spirit beings. And we do not die, as you are now aware.

Einstein pauses silently, in the beautiful and infinitely consoling realm of thought alone.

EH I sense you are deep in thought. I have always believed that thought is powerful, that thoughts are things. Each of us draws from life what we think into it. To learn how to think is to learn how to live. If you think correctly, you can bring into your experience whatever you desire. This is done by knowing the truth. We arrive, by the route of inductive science, to the great spiritual deduction of the ages — that all is one.

AE Ja, ja. You have put this in perspective for me. I am uplifted, and I thank you for your insights.

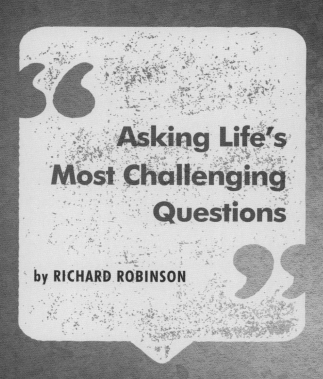

Asking Life's Most Challenging Questions

by RICHARD ROBINSON

A Conversation with Jesus Christ

PRESUPPOSE THAT AFTER JESUS WAS SEATED at the right hand of God, like the Father he ceased to speak with tongue, but as Holmes wrote, he spoke "in that universal language of spiritual emotion... sense, feeling, intuition, instinct." Arriving then as he did at the Temple courtyard in the early morning of April 7, 1960, Holmes asked the gatekeeper if the Master-Teacher was in and available for an informal chat. Holmes was shown into the main assembly room for the first of many chats, invited to sit with Jesus himself. Here starts a dialogue of cosmic importance.

ERNEST HOLMES I have been anticipating our meeting for some time. I have a short list of questions I have been working with myself and would greatly appreciate your input. When you first formed your band of followers and those 12-plus practitioners, did you have concerns about keeping your teachings pure? Did you first enroll them in your 10 key concepts?

EH Did you ever think that you hadn't made your core teachings clear, simple, direct enough that they would be easily accessible, used, demonstrated? I wish I had asked for a rewrite on some passages of my textbook. I could have expressed some things clearer than I did back in 1926. Oh well! We do our best in the moment to explain complex theological concepts. I probably could have leaned a little more on Love, as you did so well. Those of us who followed your teachings closely knew that you had created a great New Beginning and a Truth teaching. Several of us in New Thought metaphysics attempted to take your words further into the full realization of our Divinity. I really wish you had been given more time on the earth-plane to teach us. But by your leaving us, we received the awareness that our personal salvation was truly an "inside job." Your words led the way.

EH Here's the kicker: When you talk to God, whom you call The Father, when you tune into The Indwelling Holy Spirit, do you get an audible response or just an intuitive hit? You know sometimes the response comes to me loud and clear, and other times It is so quiet nobody could hear, not even a whisper. I really want to talk with you about the Lazarus effect and some of those other powerful demonstrations of faith — the loaves and fishes, turning water to wine. You see, I like demonstrations, too. But I see our shared time is coming to a close today.

EH Lastly, when did you become aware that there would be many pathways to God, many variations of faith all leading us to our oneness with God? We still struggle with that algorithm.

EH I do hope that we can continue these talks soon, I have so much to ask and to tell you about also. Right now I need to wander around, get my bearings and become acquainted with this new expression of Life. And I am off to find my best friend, an earlier check-in here, my wonderful partner and wife Hazel. Have you by chance seen her around?

"One day [my German Shepherd] Prince and I were in the garden, watching a caterpillar. The caterpillar was in our world yet in his own dimension, inching along, his mind preoccupied with caterpillar worries, whatever they may be. I knew something about his future, however, and in the long view he was in better shape than he suspected. Some instinct would take him out of the cold weather and into a cocoon. ... He'd take it for granted, of course, but he'd be a butterfly soaring over a sunlit garden. If a law does this for an insect, what d'you suppose it does for the higher consciousness of man? I can't help being curious about it, Bill. It's sure to be an improvement. I've always known that. I was born knowing it."

"The Inner Light: Delightful Reflections from
the Life of Dr. Ernest Holmes"
by William H.D. Hornaday and Harlan Ware

" Taking to the Road

by MARILYN LEO "

A Conversation with Richard Leo

RICHARD LEO OFTEN ACTED AS CHAUFFEUR for Ernest Holmes

when traveling to the Asilomar conference or on other long trips.

RICHARD LEO Good morning, Ernest. Ready for Tijuana this morning? You always enjoy our trips south of the border.

ERNEST HOLMES Good morning, Richard. You're bright and early for our outing today.

RL I look forward to seeing if I can keep up with you today.

EH I do have lots of energy and love to bargain with the Mexican vendors. I think they, too, enjoy the bargaining.

RL I know you do. I just don't know how you keep going at such a fast pace.

EH I seem to remember that we teach something about that. The energy of God is my energy, and there is no limit to the supply.

RL I know we teach that, but I get tired just trying to keep up with you.

EH I get lots of practice teaching five or more classes a week — plus Sundays and board meetings. It gets to be a bit much, but these times when we can get away are helpful, especially our conferences.

RL Yes, I love Asilomar and interacting with the youth. Do you remember the time when one our youth leaders, Roger Harrison,* became so sick with that high fever?

EH Yes, indeed. I stayed with him for a while and did spiritual mind treatments.

RL It was wonderful, Ernest. He was up and about the next day.

EH Well of course. I would not have expected anything different. I love the young people and I love our teaching. There could only be healing.

* Note from Marilyn Leo: Years later Roger Harrison told me that after that episode of rheumatic fever he had only one more bout during his life. He became one of our ministers.

The following is an excerpt
of an actual conversation with Ernest, as told in
"The Inner Light: Delightful Reflections from the Life of Dr. Ernest Holmes"
by William H.D. Hornaday and Harlan Ware

"Do you really love everybody?" [Holmes] asked, looking directly into my eyes. "Do you really bless them that persecute you?"

"I try," I said stoutly, and succumbed to a fit of coughing.

He had been concerned that morning because I had the symptoms of a cold.

"You are not angry at anyone?" he asked. "Sometimes emotional stress causes a cold. Is it not true?"

That, too, was a new idea — new to me, but 4,000 years old to the Chinese.

Gently he suggested that I join him in a Buddhist service. Honestly believing that the wrath of God would be upon me, I declined.

He was philosophical. "Yet, it is our duty to take note of how we feel within ourselves about ourselves and about others," he told me gently. "When this has been done properly, we find ourselves in perfect balance."

I assured him that I felt all right, really I did. ...

"When you have forgiven yourself and others, when you have recognized that all life is God, that that life is within you, then you can bring the blocks together in wholeness; you will feel better, and life henceforth will be more meaningful."

It was an hour that would be with me from then on; it was the first time I had been called upon to do for myself the things I'd prayed that God would do for me.

Awakening Humanity to Our Challenges

by ROGER W. TEEL

A Conversation with Tenzin Gyatso, His Holiness, the Fourteenth Dalai Lama

IF DR. ERNEST HOLMES HAD A BRIEF CONVERSATION WITH TENZIN GYATSO, His Holiness the Fourteenth Dalai Lama, it might go something like this. Direct quotes from these luminaries are shown in italics.

ERNEST HOLMES   Your Holiness, I have long admired Buddhism, especially for its deep examination of the mind and the power of thought. In "The Science of Mind," we help people understand the limitless potential within them, and this starts by working constructively in Mind.

DALAI LAMA   Thank you, and I agree. The Buddha proclaimed: *All that we are arises with our thoughts. With our thoughts we make our world.*

EH   Yes, and it seems most essential to dissolve thoughts of separation and to build up an awareness of oneness. *The power in all religions is in the spiritual principles involved and in our conscious unity with these principles…. We are members of everyone's religion. Buddhist, Confucian, Muslim, Jew, Christian and even pagan — all partake of the same Divine Life; each has his road to Good, to the divine that is latent within everyone.*

DL   This is a most powerful approach. For years I have sought to awaken humanity to the critical challenges we face: erosion of the earth's ecology … education for all … the gap between rich and poor … reviving practices of nonviolence … and harmony among religions. Moreover, we must teach and practice compassion. *We can reject* *everything else: religion, ideology, all received wisdom. But we cannot escape the necessity of love and compassion. This, then, is my true religion, my simple faith…. Our own heart, our own mind, is the temple. The doctrine is compassion.*

EH So true! *We are on the verge of a great spiritual awakening.... The world is undergoing the death throes of an old order and the travail of a new birth … and whether or not it remains suspended in a state of indeterminate coma or passes immediately into the Heaven of divine promise will depend entirely upon how many of its ancient corpses it is willing to lose. It is as certain as that the laws of nature are immutable, that someday the world will be reborn, resurrected into a consciousness of unity, cooperation, love and collective security.*

DL May we honor one another deeply . . . and do this great work together.

Developing Our Consciousness

by NADIA OHAR

A Conversation with The Voice

WHILE MANY THINK OF A VOICE from beyond as a conscience or a comfort, in this conversation Ernest talks with a voice that asks him to probe more deeply.

ERNEST HOLMES The day was warm and breezy with just the right ambiance that led me to sit with my back pressed against the tree. From this one solid form emerged limbs with branches going in all different directions. With my eyes closed I reflected on how this one tree revealed so many aspects of life. The branches deliberately went their own way, making room for the others, but carrying their own leaves. They seemed to be in harmony with each other, and in their being I sensed a peace that relaxed me even more.

THE VOICE Why is it that prayers seem to work for some people but not for others?

EH I let the question resonate within me before I began to answer.

EH We all have a consciousness that needs to be developed into a strong belief system that supports the idea that life is good and that we are all deserving of this good. When prayers are needed they will be answered according to individual faith and belief. It is not through pleading or pretending it might happen, but because of the thankfulness that it has already been done according to your belief. Prayer is never at fault. The conditioning of your mind brings your effect.

THE VOICE How can many people look at one situation and not see the same thing?

EH Perception is at the core of belief. Just like there are two sides to a coin; it is still the same coin. For instance, I might look at a warm sunny day as a chance to step out into the glorious sunshine, feeding off the rays of the sun like a plant getting ready to bloom. Someone else might perceive the day as hot, sticky and humid and worry about getting sunburned. Same day, but two ways of looking at the same situation. Whatever our minds are conditioned to see, we will see it that way. You can change your thinking to change your life.

THE VOICE I understand it's wrong to judge others but what is the difference between judging and having an opinion?

EH I would like to say that I believe opinions do not get stuck in "holding cells" the way judgments do. Opinions change, whereas judgments seem to stick to the object or person being judged. Observations tend to be healthy, but judgments tend to have a negative quality because criticism and judgment are closely related. I think the acorn had the opportunity to grow into something magnificent because there were no judgments placed on it. We are the same as the acorn in some respects because we have everything inside of us to grow into magnificence beings. The only thing that hinders our growth is the judgment placed on us. And that, my friend, is my opinion.

THE VOICE I have only one more question. If love is the answer to all problems, why isn't it used more often?

EH First of all, we are all beings of love. This is who we are, not necessarily something we use. When we are being love, it is naturally reflected back to us. If we were to use love, then that would make it manipulative and conditional. If we look at love as something outside of ourselves, then we believe we can give it or withhold it according to our selfish needs. Love is then distorted, with labels like "love hurts" or the illusion that love disappears. The truth is when you try to define love you limit its existence. Just like the branches of a tree cannot be contained in the trunk of the tree but expand outwardly, so is true of love. Having said that I will end by saying that love is and you are. And so it is.

Understanding Transition

by RICK MORGAN

A Conversation with Rick Morgan

I HAVE THIS FAVORITE ROCK on a wooded knoll. You can look through the trees out at the cove in front of our house. I spend much time in this spot, on this rock, by myself. It is my sanctuary, looking at the calm water of the cove that reflects the house where so much confusion lives. I am 9; my mother just died. On this particular day, I walk my bicycle up the hill to my favorite rock. I find a stranger sitting on my rock. I approach apprehensively. His back to me, he turns and greets me by name.

ERNEST HOLMES Hi, Rick, I have been waiting for you. My name is Ernest. I hope you don't mind me intruding on your space for a moment?

RICK MORGAN How do you know my name?

EH Well, it is kind of difficult to explain. Do you have a moment? I think you will be able to understand the explanation. You come here often and talk to God, right?

RM Yes.

EH This is your secret place, no one knows you're here, and you get to think quietly and ask questions to God with out any interruptions. But it seems that your questions go unanswered, or so you think.

RM Yeah, why doesn't God answer me? Or make things better? I wonder if anyone listens to me at all.

EH That's why I am here. Now you can ask your questions to someone directly, and hopefully I will be able to answer them so you no longer feel that way.

RM So did God send you to answer my questions?

EH What do you think?

RM I am beginning to think so, but can that be? So God is listening to me? How can he hear me over all the people that must be talking to him?

EH That's a good question, Rick. Most people would like to know how and if God can hear them. Let's see if I can explain it so it makes sense to you.

Let me start by helping you to understand God. God is divine intelligence in the form of pure positive energy that can't really be seen but can be felt. God is the source of everything. Let's call God "Source," since God is the creator of everything, would you agree?

RM Yeah.

EH See all those beautiful white puffy clouds in the blue sky, see these trees and the water that surrounds us here? Source created all these things to experience, in physical form, what could not be experienced as pure positive energy. Is this making any sense to you?

RM I think so. So God is not a man in the sky looking down on us, telling us what to do and punishing people who are bad?

EH Some people believe that. But in reality, there is no being standing in judgment. See, pure positive energy is also known as love. So you know what that means? It means not only are you love, you are loved no matter what you do, it is unconditional. That is what Source is, and what you are.

RM Then why do I feel so sad, if I am part of God, if I am love?

EH Because you have not been able to make that connection with the Source part of you. Rick, you miss your mother since she transitioned, right?

RM You mean since she died?

EH Yes, but since we are all connected with God, she didn't die. Her body died, and she made the transition to pure positive energy. Her energy is now not only all around you but part of you. Actually, she is closer to you now than she was in her physical body.

Rick, when you love someone, you want them to be happy, and you care when they are not. Know, my friend, she is happy now. She is complete pure positive energy. She is love in it's purest form. And she is now filling you with that love. How does that make you feel, knowing that?

RM I feel good knowing that.

As I sat and listened I could feel a feeling I had never felt before fill me, and I started to cry. I didn't totally understand all of this but something strong filled me, and I just knew that what he was saying was the truth.

Finding Expansion in Divine Discontent

by MARY JOY DONOVAN

A Conversation with God Himself

WHEN THE PEARLY GATES of heaven opened wide to admit Ernest Holmes, he went straight to the Source and arranged an immediate audience with God Himself.

GOD HIMSELF Well done, Ernest. You have expressed with such clarity and eloquence the ancient parables of Jesus in modern-speak so that men and women could see the Light causing them to change their ways and to come unto me. Tell Me, what have you to say for yourself?

ERNEST HOLMES It was not I but my followers who did all the works; and bless them, they continue doing all these works even today. Of myself, I did nothing except what any spiritual scholar would do — write, teach and share all Your secrets of the laws of life and how to use them.

GOD Modest, as ever. Out of nothing has come a worldwide teaching that is changing the lives of millions. I call that a "big" nothing.

EH Ah, gosh, God, You know they are all my brothers and sisters, and I so wanted to help them. It really was nothing — I couldn't even stop myself. You kept nagging until I had no choice but to go on. But I would do it all over again if You said the word.

GOD Nagging? I call this nagging by a loftier name befitting my stature in this world of Mine — divine discontent. Don't you think that name is trendy even today?

EH Well, God, I'll grant you that. You've got that one grandfathered in all right. But I must confess, it didn't feel like it was too divine at the time.

GOD Well said, Ernest. I'll think it over until I'm ready to speak my word. By the way, what's that "Game of Life" all about?

EH It isn't a board game, God. It's a mental "gotcha" game played out in an individual's thought life, being ignorant of Your laws — and meeting comeuppance at the hands of cause and effect, which claims ignorance is no excuse.

GOD That's too bad, but self-choice is freedom.

EH Freedom, God? Not when the rules of the game are cloaked in secrecy.

GOD I see. I'll think on that, too. Tell Me, why did you decide to study the ancient parables?

EH I noticed in Bible classes the students always asked questions about parables, like: Huh? What? What did that mean? What'd he say? So I decided to study the parables myself and find out their secrets, mostly out of curiosity but also for extra credits.

GOD I admire your candor, Ernest. Glad it was rewarding for every-one. Gotta go now: I've got a real cool black hole opening tonight, and I don't want to miss it. Nice chatting with you.

EH Likewise. I'll be around, if You come up with anything. Just don't keep it a secret! Let there be word sent to me.

"I have had one obsessive desire since we founded our church:
to prove to men and women that true science and
true religion are not at variance.
That each individual can attune himself to the God
Consciousness within and find the answer
to all his needs and aspirations."

Dr. Ernest Holmes, as quoted in
"In His Company: Ernest Holmes Remembered"
by Marilyn Leo

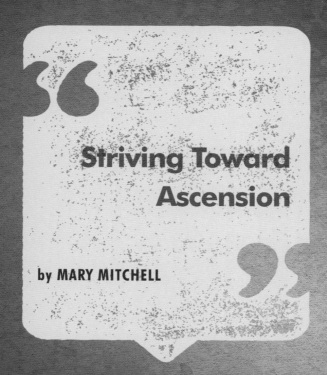

Striving Toward Ascension

by MARY MITCHELL

A Conversation with a Man Imprisoned for Murder, Dr. Michael Nichols

Writer's Note: In 2009, Dr. Michael Nichols, in a Missouri prison for murder, saw my name in Creative Thought Magazine and wrote to me, asking if I would help him study the Science of Mind. He thought there might be something in it that could help him understand his life. Since that time, his evolution of consciousness has been profound. The writings below by Dr. Nichols are in his own words.

THE MEETINGS BETWEEN HOLMES AND NICHOLS COULD HAVE TAKEN PLACE in the Southeast Correctional Institution in Charleston, Missouri.

MICHAEL NICHOLS (2010) Putting the Science of Mind into practice in prison is challenging. Every year, month, week and day is the facsimile of the last. I'm alive, yet humans encased in concrete are like the living dead, oscillating between the past and the future. The present is where most do not want to be, so we give up that which we do not possess … our future. It is taken before it has even been touched. One who cannot see the end of his existence is not able to aim at an ultimate goal in life, but something calls me to your teaching.

ERNEST HOLMES While bondage is an experience, there is a Reality in which bondage is not real. Limitation is in the individual use we make of Principle. We cannot demonstrate beyond our ability to provide a mental equivalent of our desire.

MN (2012) I've been in solitary confinement for a minor infraction with a guard who believed his clothes gave him superhuman powers. During that time I read "This Thing Called You" and learned much about the world in which I dwell. I have been made ready for the part I must play in discovering my purpose of existence. I have accepted the calling.

Recently a guard verbally attacked me for having blue shoelaces on my shoes and was shocked when I found the inner strength to take the shoelaces out and give them to him. Now, because of my action, mystery has been added to my reputation, and I'm even more frightful by virtue of my new unpredictability. It has taken courage, faith and flexibility to grow in this labyrinth of steel, yet I have come to terms with who I am. The power of a committed mind exceeds any other force that I have come across in these lands.

EH Your mind is as infinite as your capacity to understand your true relationship to God or Spirit. No form is permanent. The Formless is eternal. The will of Spirit is peace, clear thinking and happiness. It could have no other will.

MN (2013) How I value these lands where I have evolved. Today my status is as an individual connected to other individuals. I don't glamorize the ruthless prison lifestyle, but I understand. My life is connected with others even though they seem separate. My life is necessary to others.

EH To help those in need is indeed a great privilege, but the blind cannot lead the blind.

MN (2014) Your teachings have been a momentous advancement in my studies. I now have access to knowledge I had acquired only in the form of axioms. A working knowledge of the law of cause and effect has rectified my thinking. Today I value my path regardless of the hardships or the length of time it takes. I dedicate myself to Universal Mind and use the gifts I have been endowed with to build wisdom and progress to a higher level of existence, for my very soul is striving toward ascension and a transcendent understanding of creation.

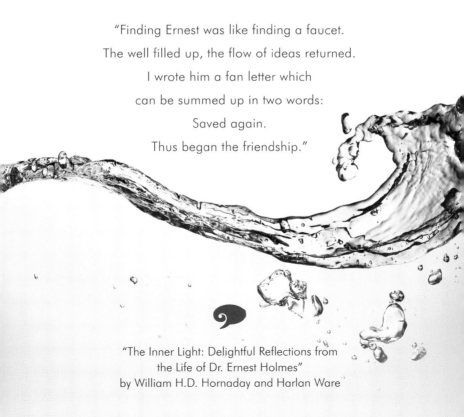

"Finding Ernest was like finding a faucet.
The well filled up, the flow of ideas returned.
I wrote him a fan letter which
can be summed up in two words:
Saved again.
Thus began the friendship."

"The Inner Light: Delightful Reflections from
the Life of Dr. Ernest Holmes"
by William H.D. Hornaday and Harlan Ware

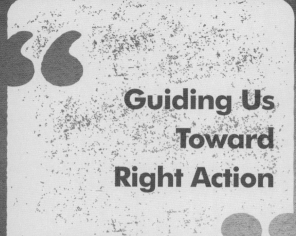

Guiding Us Toward Right Action

by JOY KREJCAREK

A Conversation with The Gull

ERNEST HOLMES BELIEVED IN THE SACRED NATURE of all life. In the following conversation, he talks with a gull about his own challenges.

THE GULL After all the successes in your life, why are you once again frozen in time?

ERNEST HOLMES I know God is living in me as guidance, right decision, strength and wisdom to succeed yet again. Knowing all of this is helpful but not the answer in real time.

GULL Do you think the past still has a hold on you?

EH Oh yes, of course. The learned responses, the learned failures, the automatic reflexes in response to flashbacks, the negative feedback. It has to be incorporated into my psyche as past history. Once again then with God's guidance and strength, which is from within, I will move.

GULL Where will you move?

EH Well, this is my dilemma. Patience or lack thereof. The churning inside saying I must move, I must take action, I must be doing. I had a goal for some time and came so close to reality in form. I was led to believe I could nourish people, heal people and give practical and spiritual advice, counsel. I have it all inside of me, so much, so much study and living of Religious Science — so much growth through God within, so much that took me through trauma after trauma.

GULL Then why aren't you achieving?

EH I have. I have achieved greatly with what I have been able to heal and accomplish. Now I have come to the latter part of my life, and I still look for more fulfillments, still look to challenge the mind.

GULL Do you realize that much of what we see with our eyes, think of with our mind is an illusion? Is it not Spirit within guiding you?

EH Yes, but the fight is on. The fight, or is flight? The churning inside that I must be doing, creating. This searching for more, this desire to achieve more, it is a good thing, is it not?

GULL Do you think that this quiet time could be filled with God's guidance into success in a different way? Are you not looking to see if you might express yourself in another area besides music, like painting?

EH Yes, but I don't believe I can write, I don't believe I can paint. However, I am taking steps to learn both avenues. Then, although it seems forever chanted that I am ageless, I am timeless. Lately, the large number of chronological age is niggling at the corners of my mind. I don't have time to continue to experiment on what I should do the remaining days. I must know just what is mine to achieve in my remaining days.

GULL Perhaps you are at a time in life that you do not need to be physically moving, involved, busy busy busy. Do you think a change is here?

EH It is still somewhat of a residue, this split personality. Listening to the Spirit guidance within motivates me, gets me to work on a plan — a plan for a physical building that has a place to live and room downstairs to open up a center, as I so want to do.

GULL What is stopping you?

EH I got stopped by a real issue in real time. A failure from a few years ago is keeping me from the means to acquire this building.

GULL Are you certain that is the answer?

EH Well, not all of it. I began to doubt and question my worth, my value. How do I think I could do this and keep it going? I cannot speak well, even if I can write well and express myself in music. Shortly thereafter, I got word that because of this, a glitch in a decision would keep me from getting the money to acquire this location.

GULL Do you think perhaps Spirit God is telling you to change your plan? Do you remember some of the affirmations that have guided you through many seemingly insurmountable challenges? Like: "This — or something better, God."

There is a statement I remember you making for many years, that when you seem frozen in time, move your feet. It doesn't have to be a giant gallop, do you remember?

EH Yes, and perhaps the completion of "the book" may be it. I will remind myself that God within guides me to my highest good; that my faith is strong, my guidance clear, my path easy.

Creating a Path to Wellness, to Love

by MARISA DIMARTINO

A Conversation with Micah

ON THIS FINAL DAY OF INDIAN SUMMER I set out to the beach one last time. As I placed my chair as close to the shore as possible could, I sensed a shadow to the right of me. When I turned to look at who was next to me, I was pleased to see a familiar face, Micah, one of the frozen snack vendors who walked the beach every day. Although we had exchanged a few pleasantries, we had never gotten into deep conversations, but there seemed to be a connection between us nonetheless. Today, however, Micah needed someone to talk to, and he knew in his heart that the conversation he needed to have could only be exchanged with me, Ernest Holmes.

MICAH Ernie, what do you think is the true meaning of love? Are we just here to experience brief moments of emotional bliss or heartache, or does it mean something more?

ERNEST HOLMES Micah, that's a great question. What I've come to understand is that love is not only what we are able to feel emotionally, but love is the essence of life and creation and the force back of everything in the Universe. It is the thread that weaves everything into and out of existence in a cyclical fashion, yet each strand is imbued and permeated with the essence of the Divine we often call God All is the Divine, and love is all it knows, gives, creates and receives.

M Wow, I've never thought of love that way. So if love is all, through all, then it's safe to say that "all" is perfect?

EH Indeed, Micah.

M So if everything is perfect, then why is there so much suffering in the world? Let me go deeper by asking why there is so much physical suffering. Why are there so many diseases that plague humanity?

EH I've wondered about that myself for many years now. I believe that what ends up being our health problems is more about the thoughts that inevitably tear us away from having balance in our spirit, which ultimately causes our diseases. Now let's look at that word and rearrange it. Dis-ease, what does that look and sound like now?

M Wow, Ernie, that's cool! So are you saying that disease is simply a lack of balance or "ease" in our daily living that it would cause everything to go off kilter?

EH Yes, Micah, indeed I'm saying that and more. I'm saying that disease is the direct result of our thinking that makes us believe in our own lack and limitation, which when ruminated over causes us strife and anxiety that ultimately translates to what causes us dis-ease or an imbalance in our spirit. This then further translates into ailments of the mind and body. I'm sure you've heard and learned that our mind and thoughts regulate a lot of our bodily functions. Likewise it would be safe to say that when our thoughts create and believe negativity, the results will always be negative. Conversely when we have positive thoughts, thoughts of goodness, wholeness and prosperity, inevitably we will have positive outcomes and our lives will be healthier.

M So are you saying we are what we think?

EH Indeed, I know that to be true.

M Does that mean we can both eliminate and prevent diseases from ever happening again or at all?

EH In all practicality, yes. Ultimately the only way to stay healthy is by thinking, believing and emulating perfect health at all times.

M So why do we need doctors and pharmaceuticals?

EH Having that option is vitally important. We're all on our own evolutionary journey, and not everyone will come to fully understand and embrace this truth. Since all things are the divine idea into form it stands to reason that all medicine and medical practices come from God and are given to us freely to better equip ourselves with what we need. It behooves us all, therefore, to appreciate and use all the medical advances of our time to our advantage and for the advancement of the human race.

M You make a great point, Ernie. I feel that if the expansion of human intellectual awareness were nonexistent, then we would be none the wiser. But what we know and have come to understand, we must put it into practice.

EH Precisely!

M I have one final question. How does all of this fit with other belief systems?

EH Well, Micah, what I've studied and witnessed and simply come to understand is that every religion or belief system is simply a path that ultimately leads to the Universal understanding that we are One. As for me, the answer is simply this: Choose any path that resonates with you. You are the Divine, and everything that God is, you also are.

M You know, Ernie, you should write this stuff down.

EH I think I just might.

Finding The Divine Golden String

by NONI BELLAND

A Conversation with The Gentle Soul

IT WAS A BEAUTIFUL DAY FOR A WALK to the neighborhood park. Ernest Holmes finds himself sitting on a bench overlooking the river below, enjoying the beauty that surrounds him. After a time, a gentle Soul walked toward him, paused, then sat down beside him. They smiled at each other and said hello. The Soul remarked how quiet and serene the day was; Ernest agreed.

THE SOUL I'm not sure why, but I had an urge to get up off my bottom and take myself outdoors. And when I saw you sitting here, I thought, "I think it's ok to sit here and chat." Although we have never met before, perhaps I can share something with you.

ERNEST HOLMES Yes, of course, how can I be of help?

SOUL I am an artist, a writer, and I am at my wit's end trying to decide what I shall write next. What will the people want from me this time? It seems that whatever I try to do, it does not get completed, and I am disappointed in myself. And my family is disappointed as well. What shall I do?

EH You have taken the next step by listening to the urge within to bring yourself outside, out into nature where you have several options — in fact, a Universe of options. You only need to listen to the small voice inside you, which whispers and whispers a little bit louder each time, until it is loud enough for you to hear, and to take action, whatever that may be.

SOUL But what? What is that 'whatever'? Can you tell me so that I am not disappointed and judged by my peers, so that I am not a failure to myself and others?

EH The first of "whatever" is already done. You brought yourself outdoors to see the next step for you. Nature has infinite opportunities. Look around here, listen to the sounds of birdsong, of the river meandering by, the sounds of the leaves in the trees when the wind rustles through. Listen and be still within you. Breathe in the fresh air, be at one with yourself, no one else. You are here, now, and you must be in this moment. No one can take this moment away from you. We are all connected together — this Nature and us.

SOUL But can you explain it a little more to me? How will I know the right thing to do, to write about?

EH If you think of a long winding golden string, going from one heart to another — through humans, animals, trees, plants — all of everything is connected together. This is the Divine Golden String, which brings us all to the realization that we are not alone, that we are all One. Feel the feeling this gives you, feel it within your heart and soul, and let go of what does not serve you, like the assumption of judgments from others. Know that all is well within you, and the feelings brought about by this meditation shall be what you write about. For example, the joy of the feeling of sunshine on your face, the sounds of the first robins in spring, and the feeling of grace and gratitude that well within your heart when you think of your loved ones, who truly do support and love, you no matter what you think. You are truly loved, and whatever you decide to write about, write it with feeling and with truth — and you will know that it is what is needed to be written.

SOUL You are just the right person for me to talk to today. I thank you for your insight, and I will take action on it and listen to those whispers more carefully, so that I may hear. And perhaps I will share them with someone else as well. I truly believe I have been given a gift of knowledge today, and I will remember it always.

"And so it is," thought Ernest. "And so it shall be."

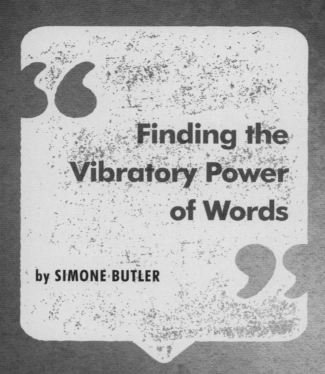

Finding the Vibratory Power of Words

by SIMONE BUTLER

A Conversation with Florence Scovel Shinn

DR. ERNEST HOLMES AND FLORENCE SCOVEL SHINN WERE INFLUENTIAL NEW THOUGHT LEADERS who came into their own in the burgeoning spiritual movement of the 1920s. Holmes came out with "The Science of Mind" in 1922; Shinn self-published her seminal work, "The Game of Life and How to Play It," in 1925. They join together here in this imagined conversation to share their thoughts on the power of words. The italicized portions are direct quotes from their writings.

ERNEST HOLMES Mrs. Shinn, I have long admired your philosophy on using the mind to create what we want. In particular, I'm impressed with the dynamic way you use words and affirmations. I have always believed that *even in the face of confusion, we can still speak a word of peace with authority because we know that behind humanity's conflicts there is always the peace of God, which is never disturbed by our strife.*

FLORENCE SCOVEL SHIN Indeed, Dr. Holmes. *The invisible forces are ever working for man who is always "pulling the strings'"himself, though he does not know it. Owing to the vibratory power of words, whatever man voices, he begins to attract.*

EH Most people do not realize what power their words carry. If you choose to demonstrate financial supply, for example, you would say, *I am surrounded by pure Spirit, perfect Law, divine order, limitless Substance, which intelligently responds to me. Daily I am guided by divine Intelligence. I am not allowed to make mistakes. I am compelled to make the right choice at the right time. There is no confusion in my mind, no doubt whatsoever. I am certain, expectant and receptive.*

FSS *Yes, words and thoughts are a tremendous vibratory force, ever molding your body and affairs. Many people have brought disaster into their lives through idle words or jokes. Be careful what you say! We must train the imaging faculty to see only good. Your clear vision must pierce the world of matter, and see the fourth dimensional world, things as they really are. Affirm, "God is my unfailing supply, and large sums of money come to me quickly, under grace, in perfect ways. I manage, spend and utilize this money in perfect ways."*

EH *When we become disturbed inside about anything, then is the moment to be still and say, "Peace!" And when we are afraid of anything, then is the time to speak the word, "Faith!" When we become angry or listen to the words of hatred, then is the moment to use the word, "Love!" It is not enough to simply speak affirmations once or twice. We must do it over and over again until what was at first a conscious and deliberate effort to speak the good word becomes so embodied in our minds, so completely accepted, that there is nothing within us that argues with the good we affirm.*

FSS Amen.

Hazel Holmes, beloved wife of Ernest,
was an animal lover. The couple enjoyed time together
in nature. The two were a beautiful pair —
Hazel in her high heels and pompadour hairstyle
never reaching taller than Ernest, always dressed in hat and gloves
as the attire of the 1920s through the 1950s.

Marilyn Leo
October 2017 issue, Guide for Spiritual Living:
Science of Mind magazine

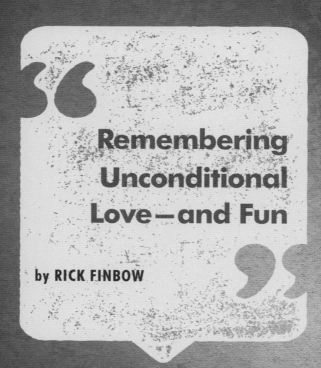

Remembering Unconditional Love—and Fun

by RICK FINBOW

A Conversation with Bella, The Beagle

BELLA FELT ANXIOUS AND EXCITED even before Ernest arrived at the door. Once there, she greeted him with many kisses. Ernest explained that it was a wonderful day outside in Colorado and asked if she would like to join him on a walk in City Park. It was just a block from Bella's home, so she agreed.

ERNEST HOLMES I would like to ask you a few questions that are of great importance to me.

BELLA, THE BEAGLE I will try to answer with openness and integrity.

EH You are a beautiful being, and I would like to first ask you of love and what it means to you.

BB Unconditional love is who I naturally am. I always come from this place. I love myself first and put others next. Love comes to me easily and in many forms. I hear the word love in my life several times a day. I am love.

EH You are such an old soul. How did you learn this?

BB I have learned love through living. Trusting others and the universe to provide, I expect the best. I have many loves and lovers. I care for them, they care for me. I show gratitude daily toward others. I let everyone know I am glad to see them and happy they are near.

EH How is your health, Bella?

BB I enjoy wonderful good health, and I am always anxious to exercise with long walks in the park and playing. We all need more playing — and more fun.

EH How does one play and have fun?

BB Anything that feels good! Playing ball with friends is still one of my favorites, even at this age. Sometimes I join young men and women playing in the park. They always laugh, giggle and applaud how agile I am. I have noticed that times have changed, and other people seem more serious and don't take as much time to unplug and just have fun. Not me, I thrive on it.

EH What about God?

BB God, as I believe, is not a person or a thing to hold onto. God is all, God is infinite, God is everything. The word God has been used in many ways. We are all from this, are made up of this, a part of it, no separation. I am God, you are God, that lovely tree over there is God, the blade of grass is God. The universe is God. God is the universe. We are all one, in and of God.

EH How did you learn this?

BB It's not something you learn. It's who we are. If I had to say where I learned more about it, I would say from you. You and others like you help me realize who I am and who I'm becoming. You, with your outstretched hand, show me trust and love. All that is God.

Bella, the beagle, made her transition in 2017 at the age of 13. Prior to that, she spent much time with Rick Finbow, who took care of her and had his own regular conversations with her. Bella knew him fondly as "Uncle Rick." Because Bella's conversation with Ernest was the first one of the series published in Guide for Spiritual Living: Science of Mind magazine, it seems only fitting that hers is the last conversation we celebrate in these pages.

BONUS SECTION

Sermon by the Sea
at Asilomar

by Dr. Ernest Holmes
Saturday, August 15, 1959

From the Science of Mind Archives and Library Foundation

573 Park Point Drive, Golden CO 80401 | www.somarchives.org | 720-496-1361

Our religion is not something to be lived merely here at Asilomar, as much inspiration as we receive from it, but rather to take that consciousness which we have arrived at here back with us into whatever activities we may be engaged in.

I do not believe Life is separated from Its living, anywhere.

There is nothing in the world that can take the place of love, friendship, appreciation and cooperation in our lives. I have thought so much about this all week because these are the only things that have any meaning in the eternal values in which we are so interested. Emerson said that it is very easy for us to maintain a spiritual equilibrium in solitude but the great man is he who in the midst of the crowds shall still keep the sweetness, the independence of his solitude.

I do not believe there is a single fact in human history or a single manifestation in the universe which is or could possibly be anything other than a manifestation of the One Divine Mind, the One Universal Presence, the One Infinite Spirit.

It seems to me that it is only as we view all life, everything from what we call great to what we call small, important or unimportant –

it is only as we view the whole thing as "one stupendous whole, whose body nature is with God the soul" that we shall really enter into communion, into sympathetic oneness and rapport, with the reality of all that is about us. Someone asked me: "What do you think God is?" I looked out the window and said, "I think God is that tree." And there was a squirrel running up the tree," and I said, "I think God is that squirrel."

It is going to be absolutely impossible for us, with our finite comprehension, to have the intelligence to divide the indivisible and to say this is real and that is unreal. The marketplace is as real as is the temple. That is why Jesus said that it is neither in the temple at Jerusalem nor in the mountain but in yourself that the secret of Life is discovered, that the Soul of the Universe is consciously entered into, and the Divine and benign Spirit which indwells everything is loosed in Its splendor and power through you – through your partnership with the Infinite, through your oneness with God, the living Spirit.

A Purpose, Consciousness, Philosophy

Everything that lives proclaims the Glory of God. Every person who exists manifests the Life of God. There is One Spirit in which we live, One Mind by which we think, One Body of which we are a part and One Light that lighteth every man's pathway.

*Ernest Holmes
as a young man*

We are a part of the evolution of human destiny; we are a part of the unfoldment of the Divine Intelligence in human affairs. It has reached the point of conscious and deliberate cooperation with that principle of evolution and out-push of the creative urge of the Spirit, on this planet at least, to bring about innumerable centers which It may enjoy. Also we may enjoy It through that Divine interior awareness which is the intercommunication of God with man, revealing our own Divine nature.

Having had the privilege of starting Religious Science, I would wish, will and desire above all things else that the simplicity and purity of our teaching could never be violated. There is a purpose of simplicity, a consciousness of unity, a straight-line thinking in our philosophy that has never appeared before in the world, outside of the teachings of men like Jesus and Emerson.

There was nothing obscure in the teaching of Jesus. He just said that is the Father's good pleasure to give you the kingdom. Why don't you take it? He said that there is nothing but God. Why don't you believe it? He was the last of the great Jewish prophets, the greatest line of emotional prophets the world has ever known.

The Greeks had the greatest intellectual perception of the ages. It appears in their literature and art – a perfect thing without a soul.

We also find a great intellectualism in Emerson, who never contradicted himself. He gave us the simplest statement of intellectual spiritual perception, probably, that has ever been put into print. As that of Jesus, it was most simple, direct, meaningful and feelingful. We inherit this.

Simplicity, Purity, Directness

It would be my desire that simplicity and purity and directness, that straight thinking, should never depart from the teachings of our practitioners, or instructions of our teachers or understanding of our laymen. It is the most direct impartation of Divine Wisdom that has ever come to the world, because it incorporates the precepts of Jesus and Emerson and Buddha and all the rest of the wise. And I would desire that in our teaching there would never be any arrogance, for that always indicates spiritual immaturity to me. Others will arise who will know more than we do; they won't be better or worse, they will be different and know more than we do. Evolution is forward.

I would desire that we should not build, out of the body of our simplicity and grandeur and beauty, other creeds loaded with superstition, a fear of the unknown and a dread of the unseen. We have discovered a pearl of great price; we have discovered the rarest

gem that has ever found setting in the intellect of the human race – complete simplicity, complete directness, a freedom from fear and superstition about the unknown and about God.

And we have rediscovered that which the great, the good and the wise have sung about and thought about – the imprisoned splendor within ourselves and within each other – and have direct contact with it. Whether we call it the Christ in us, or the Buddha, or Atman or just the Son of God the living Spirit, makes no difference. You and I are witness to the Divine fact, and we have discovered an authority beyond our minds, even though our minds utilize it. Out of this we have prepared ourselves, I think, I hope, I pray and believe.

One cannot but feel from the human point in such meetings as these that is entirely possible one might not be here next year. This is of complete indifference to me because I believe in life, and I feel fine. Such an event is merely the climax of human events in anybody's life, and it is to be looked forward to, not with dread or fear or apprehension but as the next great adventure and one that we should all be happy and glad to experience.

But we must weigh and measure things somewhat from the human angle. No person or organization can make the provision for that which is paramount, for that which is of the most stupendous importance: that out of the ranks of all of us, innumerable people shall grow up who shall have caught a vision, who shall have seen a glory, who shall have experienced God.

The Savior Within

The thing that interests me now is that every man shall find his savior within himself. If this is the only place he is going to discover God, you may be sure it is the only avenue through which any way-shower shall lead him to God. There is no other way. Jesus knew this, and when they sought to make Jesus, the man, the way, he said that it was expedient he go away that the spirit of Truth should awaken within his followers the knowledge and understanding of what he had been talking about – that he had come to reveal them to themselves.

As we think, speak, talk and commune with each other and with nature and God, there will never be an answer to us beyond the level of our approach. The level of our approach is the only avenue through which there could be an answer, else we would not be individuals. God cannot make a mechanical spontaneity, and that is why we are left alone to discover ourselves.

Those who bear witness in consciousness do not need to retire from life. The great man is he who, in the midst of the crowd, can

Radio broadcasts, including
"This Thing Called Life," drew a wide audience
of people interested in his teachings

keep with perfect simplicity the independence of his solitude. It is not in the mountain or the temple in Jerusalem; it is in our own heart, our own mind, our own consciousness, our own being, where we live 24 hours a day, awake or asleep, that that eternal share of the Infinite comes to us, because every man is some part of the essence of God, not as a fragment, yet as totality.

I think we have brought a blessing to the world, the possibility of something expressing through us that has never before been given to the world – a simplicity, a sincerity and, I trust, a love and understanding. But we too little practice it because the human mind is prone, even when it has discovered a greater good than it had before, to compare the degree of good it thinks it possesses with a lesser degree of good it thinks someone else has. And this is brought about only through the psychological projection of some unredeemed past of a person's own psyche.

You will never discover a person who is full of emotional judgment and condemnation of others who is doing anything other than unconsciously releasing the tension of a burden – a burden so great to be borne that he does not even permit it to come to the light of day to be seen, for he could not face it. This has been scientifically proved, and that is why Jesus, with the profoundness of utmost simplicity, did not say: Judge not lest God will judge you. He knew better. He said: "Judge not, that ye be not judged. For with what judgment ye judge, ye shall be judged." In other words, your judgment will judge you. "And with what measure ye mete, it will be measured to you again." God is not going to measure it back to you and say: I will show you who is boss. You are the measure-outer. As Troward said, we are dispensers of the Divine Gift, and we are in partnership with the Infinite.

Find Me Someone

It would be wonderful indeed if a group of persons should arrive on earth who were for something and against nothing. This would be the sum of human organization, wouldn't it? It is, in the life of the individual.

Find me one person who is for something and against nothing, who is redeemed enough not to condemn others out of the burden of his soul, and I will find another savior, another Jesus and an exalted human being.

Find me one person who no longer has any fear of the universe, or of God, or of man or of anything else, and you will have brought to me someone in whose presence we may sit, and fear shall vanish as clouds before the sunlight.

William Hornaday
with Holmes

Find me someone who has redeemed his own soul, and he shall become my redeemer.

Find me someone who has given all that he has in love, without morbidity, and I will have found the lover of my soul. Is not this true? Why? Because he will have revealed to me the nature of God and proved to me the possibility of all human souls.

This is what Religious Science stands for. It is not a new dogmatism, it is not a new authority generated from a new alleged revelation of the God who never revealed anything to anybody, as such, else He could not have revealed all things to all people. There is no special dispensation of Providence, but there is a specialized dispensation which the great and good and wise and just have known, even though they knew it intuitively.

Find me one person who can get his own littleness out of the way, and he shall reveal to me the immeasurable magnitude of the Universe in which I live.

Find me one person who knows how to talk to God, really, and I shall walk with him through the woods. And everything that seems inanimate will respond – the leaves of the trees will clap their hands, the grass will grow soft under him.

Find me one person who communes with cause and effect, and in the evening, the evening star will sing to him and the darkness will turn to light. Through him, as the woman who touched the hem of the garment of Christ was healed, shall I be healed of all loneliness forever.

Find me someone who is no longer sad, whose memory has been redeemed from morbidity and I shall hear laughter.

Find me someone whose song is really celestial, because it is the outburst of the cosmic urge to sing and I shall hear the music of the spheres.

"All things are delivered unto me of my Father: and no man knoweth the Son but the Father; neither knoweth any man the Father, save the Son and he to whomsoever the Son will reveal him." And each of us is that Son. No use waiting for avatars. Jesus is not coming again – he is wiser than that. He has earned whatever he has. And to you and to me no single kernel of grain shall come unless we have planted it, no meal shall be made unless we have ground it, no bread baked unless we have kneaded it and put it in the oven of our own consciousness where the silent processes of an invisible and ineffable light precipitates itself into that which for us stands for the start of life.

But how we have put off that day! We say to each other that we don't know enough, we aren't good enough. The ignorance of our

*A birthday celebration
with Janet Gaynor*

unknowing, the blindness of our unseeing, the condemnation of the ages weighing against our consciousness, known and unknown, conscious and unconscious, has created the greatest possibility of the larger progress of humanity a burden so tremendous that even men's adoration of God has been saddened by fear. Like the man who Newman said prayed, "O God, if there be a God, save my soul, if I have a soul." He did not know so was afraid to take a chance.

Find me one person who no longer doubts, no longer waivers. But not one who with a proclamation of superiority says: Look at me, I have arrived! I will not listen to that. Only that which reveals me to myself can be a message to me; only that which gives me back myself can save me; only that which leads me to the God within myself can reveal God. And only that person can do it to whom the vision has come through his own efforts, through the gift of God.

Of course, the grace of God abounds by Divine givingness. God has forever hung Himself upon the cross of men's indifference; God has forever, but without suffering, given Himself but we have not received the gift.

Find me one person who has so completely divorced from himself all arrogance, and you will have discovered for me an open pathway to the kingdom of God here and now. Up until now the search has been in far-off corners of the earth, and we have knelt upon a

Ernest with his mother, Anna Holmes

prayer rug and been wafted away, in our morbid and fearful imagination, over ethers of nothingness to places that have no existence, the temples of our unbelief, and we have come back empty. "What went ye out into the wilderness for to see.... "

And now comes Religious Science. We are no more sincere than others; if we felt we were that would be a projection of our insincerity. We are no better; if we thought we were that would be a projection of an unconscious sense of guilt. Anyway, it would be stupid, and there is no greater sin on earth than just plain stupidity.

What shall reveal the self to the self? The self shall raise the self by the self.

Find me somebody who has detached his emotional and psychological ego from the real self, without having to deny the place it plays in the scheme of things and without slaying any part of himself because the transcendence is there also, and I will have discovered the Ineffable in this individual and a direct pathway for the communion of my own soul.

Centered in Our Own Soul

Now what does this all mean? I am talking about you and myself. When I say "find a person" I don't mean to go over to Rome or

London or back to your own church. The search is not external. All of these people I have been talking about have no existence as such, other than as figments of my own imagination, until they are finally centered in our own soul. Then this Guest for whom we are looking will be the Self redeemed from the lesser self. This is a very interesting thing, for nature is foolproof and when the fruit is ripe it will fall; when the kingdom of God is perceived, it will be experienced simultaneously, instantaneously and in its entirety.

But these people all exist in us. They are different attributes, qualities of our own soul. They are different visions; not that we have multiple or dual personalities but that every one of us on that inner side of life is, has been and shall remain in eternal communion with the Ineffable where he may know that he is no longer with God, but one of God. If it were not for that which echoes eternally down the corridors of our own minds, some voice that ever sings in our own souls, some urge that continuously presses us forward, there would be no advance in our science or religion or in the humanities or anything else. But "….he left not himself without witness."

These are simple things that call for discipline. Not as one normally thinks of discipline, but a different kind of discipline that one discovers. I often sit for several hours at a time, sometimes all day, thinking one simple thought, no matter what it is. It isn't a waste of time to find out what this thought means to me or what it should mean in my life or what it would mean everywhere. This is something no one can do for us but ourselves. We are "the way, the truth and the life."

We have come to Asilomar, spent this wonderful week together on love for each other and adoration for the God we believe in. Many wonderful things have happened that would seem miracles if we didn't know about them. And now we meet for this fond farewell after the spiritual bath of peace, the baptism of the spirit. Not through me, but you to me and I to you through each other – the revelation of the self to the self – we go back into the highways and byways of life with something so great that never again will anything be quite the same.

A little more light shall come, a little greater glory added to the glory that we already possess, a deeper consciousness, a higher aspiration, a broader certainty of the mind.

You are Religious Science. I am not. I am only the one who put something together. I do not even take myself seriously, but I take what I am doing seriously. You are Religious Science — our ministers, our teachers, our practitioners, our laymen. You find me 1,000 people in the world who know what Religious Science is and use it and live it as it is, and I'll myself live to see a new world, a new heaven

Holmes with Cecil B. DeMille and Donald Curtis

and a new earth here. There is a cosmic Power wrapped up in a cosmic Consciousness and Purposiveness that is equal to the vision which looses It.

What I am saying is this: There is a Law that backs up the vision and the Law is immutable. "Heaven and earth shall pass away; but my words shall not pass away." There is a Power transcendent beyond our needs, our little wants. Demonstrating a dime is good if one needs it, or healing oneself of a pain is certainly good if one has it, but beyond that, at the real feast at the tabernacle of the Almighty, in the temple of the living God, in the banquet hall of heaven, there is something beyond anything that you and I have touched.

Find 1,000 people who know that and use it, and the world will no longer be famished. How important it is that each one of us in his simple way shall live from God to God, with God, in God and to each other. That is why we are here, and we are taking back with us, I trust, a vision and an inspiration, something beyond a hope and a longing that the living Spirit shall through us walk anew into Its own creation and a new glory come with a new dawn.

Now the Lord is in His holy temple. Let all the Earth keep silent before Him as we drink deep from the perennial fountain of eternal life, as we partake of the bread of heaven, and as we open wide the gates of our consciousness that the King of Glory shall come in.

And may God bless and keep us,
and for all the love you have given me,
may I bless you.

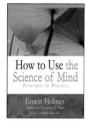

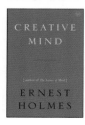

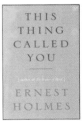

We publish *Ernest Holmes* and many more inspiring New Thought authors ...

365 Days of Richer Living: A Daily Guidebook of Powerful, Inspiring, Affirmative Prayers and Meditations (How to Use Your Mind Power)

Ernest Holmes, Lloyd Tupper, Kathy Hearn and Raymond Charles Barker

Encouraging Words: Articles and Essays That Prove Who You Are Matters

Be reminded that there lies within each of us an explorer who yearns for higher ground.

Dennis Merritt Jones

Providence: A Story of Hope

Raging planetary climate change brings mass devastation, but the universal force of love ushers humanity toward a sweeping world revolution.

June E. Summers

A Simple Guide to Planetary Transformation: How Your Personal Spiritual Journey Can Change the World

Principles, prayers and daily practices for your soul.

Gregory Toole

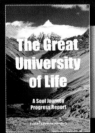

Ernest let it be known that he was not to be disturbed the first hour in the morning, as that was his time for meditation. The rest of the day and evening, he was out and about and available and made himself at home [while staying with Dorothy and Norman Lunde]. He would put on an apron he found in the kitchen and make shortcake, and over the next three weeks, whatever else he took a fancy to. One particular day he saw Dorothy outside washing the car. Since this was "man's work," he said to Dorothy, "What are you doing out there washing the car?" She said, "What are you doing in the kitchen in that frilly pink apron?" They both had a good laugh, and Ernest went outside and they sat down and talked for more than an hour.

"In His Company: Ernest Holmes Remembered"
by Marilyn Leo

Ernest and Hazel Holmes
with Peggy Lee and William Hornaday